Thank God I Failed!
Discovering the Ministry of Failure
By Carl George
Edited by Andrea Merrell

Contents

Introduction

Why is this Book Yellow?

I was excited when our church gave permission to use this book in a small group study. In preparation, I asked my wife to purchase binders and was disappointed when she brought home five yellow binders. Despite her own reservations about the color, the back-to-school rush had limited her choices. Apparently, no one else wanted yellow binders either. As I considered the reasons for my disappointment, I realized yellow would be the perfect color for my book.

Why yellow? Yellow is the color of weakness. It is the color most associated with fear and indecision, which is why someone who lacks courage is described as *yellow*. It is also the color of sunshine and happiness. It is the least respected of the three primary colors and yet, when joined with red and blue, creates stunning colors in an infinite spectrum. Without yellow, there would be no green grass or fiery sunsets. In these respects, yellow is much like failure. Failure is often equated with weakness and losing, but when failure is mixed with two other primary forces—the grace and sovereignty of God—our life story can become an unexpected tapestry of astonishing beauty.

Since beginning to write this book, I have had the pleasure of talking to and interviewing numerous people who have experienced varying degrees of failure. Many, even the most extreme examples, said they thanked God for what He had done through their failure, despite the pain. The biblical truths and life lessons in this book can help each of us experience this hope. "Thank God I Failed!" may sound like an impossible sentiment, but, as you will see, many people can testify to its reality.

This book is broken into the following sections:

Chapters One, Two and Three – definition and theological foundation for the Ministry of Failure

Chapter Four and Five – consequences of failure

Chapter Six and Seven – practical advice for avoiding unnecessary failure

Chapter Eight – personal lessons learned through failure

Chapters Nine and Ten – failure from God's perspective

After each chapter, there are questions for individual meditation or group discussion. There are also testimonies throughout this book from people who have learned tremendous lessons through the Ministry of Failure.

Much of this book contrasts the Ministry of Failure with our Culture of Success. As you consider this contrast through the lessons and testimonies in this book, you may be struck, as I have been, by the pervasive nature of both the Ministry of Failure and the Culture of Success – two powerful forces pulling our hearts in different directions. As we struggle with our own response to the reality of failure, may God grant us the powerful grace that comes from living life broken and transformed in this awareness.

Chapter One

Ministry of Failure Defined

In 1964, the Beatles came out with a song called "I'm a Loser." While the ballad tells a wonderful story about a man who lost his heart in love, the title is reminiscent of the imaginary *L* that gets painted on the forehead of anyone who has failed. It is a crimson letter we learn to hate at a very young age on the kickball field or in that dreaded math class.

I, for one, have felt that branding for months—every time I tell someone I am a *former* pastor. The stigma of failure frequently fills me with an emotional desire to defend my status, to wipe the L off by explaining why I am not currently shepherding a church. Putting aside the lies of emotional reactions and prideful defensiveness, we can be glad there is a big difference between failing and being a loser since failure colors all of our lives.

Naval Admiral William H. McRaven illustrated our universal experience of failure in his commencement address to the 2014 graduating class of the University of Texas. In his comments, he told about lessons he learned during six months of torture, otherwise known as Seal training. During this training, they endured uniform inspection several times a week. If you failed—and everyone did—you had to run fully clothed into the surf and then roll around on the beach until every part of your body was covered with sand. For the rest of the day you were cold, wet, and sandy. They called it the "Sugar Cookie."

No matter how perfectly you put your uniform on, everyone failed. Admiral McRaven said some men could not accept inevitable failure, and these men would at some point drop out. This exercise in frustration was, in fact, intended to eliminate those who were not willing to work through their frustration to learn failure's hard lessons. "It's just the way life is," said McRaven. "If you want to change the world, get over being a sugar cookie and keep moving forward." Failure happens to everyone, but it does not need to determine who we are.

In this book I use the term *failure* to refer to four different types:

- Minor, inconsequential failures we simply do our best to avoid in the future.
- Failures over which we have no control except in our reaction to any resulting consequences.
- Failures whose repetition can be avoided through additional education, training, and hard work.
- Moral failures.

Whatever form it takes, failure is seldom enjoyable. The desire to avoid or overcome it frequently drives self-improvement and human achievement. Researchers and inventors struggle through failure in pursuit of success. Students spend years pursuing advanced degrees in order to avoid it professionally. Athletes endure countless hours of grueling workouts to avoid failure and achieve success in their chosen sport.

I have spent the past thirty years trying to be fully committed and striving for success in many different roles: spouse and father, full-time student, school and Bible teacher, pastor and church planter. During these years I have seen some of the churches I started fail. I have seen people I invested my life in fall apart spiritually. Students I have loved ended up in jail or dead from drug overdoses. Most recently, a church I was shepherding closed with its members scattered to an assortment of churches in the area.

Based on my failures, some of which I will share with you in this book, there is no reason you or anyone else would want to read this book. Ironically, the person who is most qualified to write a book like this is the least likely to be enlisted by any publisher to do so. At the same time, there is a new perspective and transformation that only comes through God's life-changing ministry through failure.

This book is not about winners or losers. It is about trying a new strategy—learning from our failures and allowing God to redeem them. It is important to do so because, whether failure is personal, professional, ministerial, or moral, it is always communal. It impacts the lives of people around us and can have a devastating impact on our plans, our relationships, and our self-esteem. It is vital for our sake and the sake of our loved ones that we allow God to use our failures. When we do, it is possible for God's Ministry of Failure to have an even greater positive impact on ourselves and on those around us than so called *success* would have had.

The Ministry of Failure is God's ministry with and through our failures. As painful as failure might be, this ministry is

3

an intentional, loving expression of God's eternal plan guiding us to experience His grace, become His children, and grow in His nature. Occasionally, as we will see, there are also times when this ministry will bring glory to God by changing our world in ways we cannot imagine. In God's economy our value is determined in our relationship with Him and not by our worldly success. The fact that God loves us is more than a statement of emotional connection. It is a statement of and the source of our eternal value. We matter because God loves us, and God is willing to use anything He can to draw us and others to Himself, including failure.

The Culture of Success, on the other hand, determines our value as an individual by the size of our business, the quality of our resume, and the number of skills and accomplishments we can list on our professional networking homepage. In this culture there is little room for failure, except as a stepping stone toward ultimate success. Little room for humble, honest confession. Little room for personal value outside of performance. This culture is as old as civilization itself. If you don't enjoy its demands, you are in good company. People like Job, Moses, Joseph, Jeremiah, Jesus, and much of the early church found themselves thrust out of this culture, rejected for failing to live up to expectations diametrically opposed to biblical principles.

Consider Jesus' parable about a successful farmer. This man was so rich that he ran out of places to hold all his produce. One day as the farmer relished his wealth, planning a wonderful retirement where he could "eat, drink and be merry," God spoke. "You fool! This very night your

4

soul is required of you; and now who will own what you have prepared?" (Luke 12:20).

The man was successful, but he was also a fool. Perhaps earthly success is not always a sign of divine blessing, and failure is not always a reason for cashing in all your chips and quitting. Maybe God just wants us to learn a new strategy, a strategy based on His transforming work in our lives through the Ministry of Failure.

Mike Rowe's Story

In my opinion, you have all been given some terrible advice. And that advice is this ... "Follow your passion." Every time I watch the Oscars, I cringe when some famous movie star, trophy in hand, starts to deconstruct the secret of their success. It's always the same thing. "Don't let anyone else tell you that you don't have what it takes kid." And the ever popular, "Never give up on your dreams."

I understand the importance of persistence and the value of encouragement, but who tells a stranger to never give up on their dreams without even knowing what they are dreaming. I mean, how can Lady Gaga possibly know where your passion will lead you? Have these people never seen American Idol? Year after year, thousands of aspiring American idols show up with great expectations only to learn they don't possess the skills they thought they did. What is really amazing though is not their lack of talent (the world is full of people who can't sing), it is their genuine shock at being rejected. The incredible realization that their passion and ability have nothing to do with each other.

If we are talking about your hobby, by all means, let your passion lead you, but when it comes to making a living, it is easy to forget the dirty truth: just because you are passionate about something doesn't mean you won't suck at it. Just because you have earned your degree in your chosen field, it doesn't mean that you will find your "dream job." Dream jobs are usually just that, dreams. But their imaginary existence might just keep you from exploring careers that offer a legitimate chance to perform meaningful work and develop a genuine passion for the job you already have. Because here is another dirty truth: your happiness on the job has very little to do with the work itself.

As the host of the show *Dirty Jobs*, I remember meeting a very successful septic tank cleaner, a multimillionaire, who told me the secret to his success. "I looked around to see where everyone else was headed," he said, "and then I went the opposite way. Then I got good at my work. Then I began to prosper, and one day I realized I was passionate about other people's crap." I have heard that same basic story from welders, plumbers, carpenters, electricians, HVAC professionals, and hundreds of other skilled tradesmen who followed opportunity, not passion, and prospered as a result.

Consider the reality of the current job market. Right now, millions of people with degrees and diplomas are out there competing for a relatively narrow set of opportunities that polite society calls "good careers" and, meanwhile, employers are struggling to fill nearly 5.8 million jobs that nobody is trained to do. This is the skills gap. It's real and its cause is actually very simple. When people follow their passion, they miss out on all kinds of opportunities they didn't even know existed.

When I was sixteen, I wanted to follow in my grandfather's footsteps. He was a skilled tradesman. He could build a house without a blueprint. That was my passion, and I followed it for years. I took all the shop classes at school. I did all I could do to absorb the knowledge and skill that came so easily to my granddad. Unfortunately, the handy gene is recessive. It skipped right over me, and I struggled mightily to overcome my deficiencies … but I couldn't. I was one of those contestants on American Idol who believed his passion was enough to ensure his success. One day I brought home a sconce [candlestick holder] I had made in wood shop. It looked like a paramecium.

After a heavy sigh, my granddad gave me the best advice I have ever received. He told me, "Mike, you can still be a tradesman, but only if you get yourself a different kind of toolbox." At the time, this felt contrary to everything I believed about the importance of passion and persistence and staying the course, but of course he was right. Staying the course only makes sense if you are headed in a sensible direction, and while passion is way too important to be without, it is way too fickle to follow around. Which brings us to the final dirty truth: never follow your passion, but always bring it with you.

Author's Note: Mike Rowe is a TV host for the show *Dirty Jobs*, writer. narrator, producer, actor and spokesman. This testimony was written for and produced in a video by PragerUniversity.com and is used with permission.

Meditation Moment

- What has driven you to read this book? Learning from failure is not usually easy. Are you willing to bring your passion to this journey even if the journey takes you places you never intended to go?

- Our experience of failure is both individual and corporate, and its expressions are extremely diverse. You may relate to some of the testimonies in this book and not to others. While some of these examples are fairly extreme, they each capture the universal human condition in some way. Are you open to looking beyond the individual circumstances and humbly applying the principles learned for yourself?

- Military men in Seal training who allow their "sugar cookie" failure to overcome them risk a possible lifetime of being haunted by the experience. Men who keep going forward become warriors. Are you willing to do what it takes to keep moving forward no matter how painful the journey may be?

Chapter Two

Power is Perfected in Weakness

We often flee from Jesus because of failure's shame when He wants most to draw near and embrace us in His love's compassion.

Do you feel like a failure? You are not alone. Even Jesus knew the pain of failure. For three years He gave Himself fully, heart and soul, to disciple twelve men. He chose them. He trained them. He served them, modeling a giving, loving, and unselfish spirit. Even though He was perfect, He failed to get His small congregation of disciples to understand the life-changing truths He taught and lived. While the source of this failure was in the disciples and not in Jesus, we find hope that Jesus knows what we are going through. In His relationship with His disciples, Jesus experienced firsthand the pain and frustration of failure. These experiences with human temptations, limitations, and failures, in fact, are at the center of one of the great truths in the Bible: "For we do not have a high priest who cannot sympathize with our weaknesses, but One who has been tempted in all things as we are, yet without sin" (Hebrews 4:15).

Our exploration of Jesus' experience with our limitations begins with the very beginning of His ministry. As John Galsworthy once wrote, "beginnings are always messy." Whether you are beginning a business, a family, or a new life direction, things seldom go as planned. The beginning of Jesus' ministry was no exception, starting in a truly spectacular fashion but quickly taking a confusing turn.

Jesus' public ministry launched when He was baptized by His cousin John. As Jesus came out of the waters of baptism, a powerful vision of glory filled the sky. Out of that vision, a lone dove flew down and gently landed on Jesus, filling Him with the abiding affirmation and anointing of the Holy Spirit. After the dove came down, the thunderous voice of His Father announced, "This is My beloved Son, in whom I am well-pleased" (Matthew 3:13-17).

You couldn't ask for a more meaningful and beautiful beginning. The Father, Son, and Holy Spirit, all giving testimony to the start of a world-changing ministry. Jesus had to be excited, but teaching, healing, raising the dead, and changing the world had to wait since God had one more baptism for Jesus to go through—a baptism in the fires of temptation.

It wasn't Jesus' idea. The Bible says, "Jesus was led up by the Spirit into the wilderness to be tempted by the devil" (Matthew 4:1).

In this call to the wilderness, Jesus experienced the same surprise many of us have felt as we follow God. His Spirit sometimes takes us places we would never dream of going.

My wife, Jacqueline, and I once experienced this surprise after her parents blessed us with a gift of a tremendous vacation. On that trip, we had a layover in Salt Lake City. Anyone who has flown into SLC in the daytime knows the airport is surrounded by factories. It's definitely not the most attractive airport setting in the world. I remember looking out the window of the plane and thinking, *God, I hope I never live here.* One year later to the day, we were on our way to our new home just north of Salt Lake City.

Was Jesus caught off guard, like we were, when the Spirit gave Him His new direction? He'd waited His whole life for this moment, and now the Spirit tells Him to go off by himself to a desolate place. What kind of ministry could He have to scorpions and snakes? As He considered turning into or away from the wilderness, could this have been the first time He had to say the prayer He would one day pray in the Garden in Gethsemane? "Not as I will, but as You will" (Matthew 26:39).

For forty days and forty nights Jesus fasted in the wilderness, which left Him physically, mentally, and emotionally exhausted. While He was in this weakened state, the tempter came, tempting Him physically with food, emotionally with affirmation and glory, and spiritually with false worship.

Why did God lead Jesus into this nightmarish experience? We know Jesus stood strong on God's Word and successfully weathered every temptation. Was the whole experience simply divine role-playing in order to model how we can resist temptation? If so, there is a problem. His temptations were unique. I don't know of anyone who has ever experienced the magnitude of temptation Jesus faced. Surely, there had to be more to the experience than just showing how successful and strong Jesus was with the hope that we could somehow live up to His example. As we consider the reason for this unexpected detour, it is important to remember that it must have been God's priority since the wilderness experience was the very first thing Jesus was led to do in ministry.

After passing through each temptation, Jesus selected His disciples and began traveling the region teaching. It did not take long for word to get around that exciting, amazing things were happening, and the crowds following Him grew explosively fast. It wasn't all a bed of roses, however. Jesus had his fair share of enemies who also followed Him around, waiting and scheming to discredit Him. While these men were undoubtedly a constant source of frustration, Jesus' greatest struggle was clearly not the spies and enemies who opposed Him. Instead, it was in the failure of His disciples to understand the truths He was trying to teach them.

In Matthew 20, for example, James and John's mother (the original career coach) appealed to Jesus for her sons to sit on thrones by His side in His earthly kingdom. No one knows whether James and John *humbly* sent her or if they just allowed their mother to seek a new exalted position for them. Whichever is the case, they clearly failed to understand Jesus' teachings on humility and service.

After talking to James and John, Jesus called all His disciples together and told them if they wanted to be great they had to follow His example and be servants, "just as the Son of Man did not come to be served, but to serve, and to give His life a ransom for many" (Matthew 20:28). James and John thought following Jesus was an avenue for worldly success, but Jesus had called them to a life of humble service.

James and John weren't the only ones to misunderstand what following Jesus was all about. After Jesus miraculously fed four thousand families, He asked His disciples who people thought He was. Peter responded boldly that Jesus was the Christ, the Son of the Living God. Jesus then gave Peter a powerful affirmation of His own.

And Jesus said to him, "Blessed are you, Simon Barjona ... I also say to you that you are Peter, and upon this rock I will build My church; and the gates of Hades will not overpower it. I will give you the keys of the kingdom of heaven." (Matthew 16:17-19)

Peter had to be on cloud nine. It was amazing praise. I am sure Peter had no idea exactly what these words meant (people still debate their meaning today), but whatever they meant, it was clear Peter's position in the coming kingdom was secure. He was to be a man of authority. It wasn't long, however, before things would change drastically.

Immediately after this declaration, Jesus began telling his followers how He had to go to Jerusalem, die, and rise from the dead. From our perspective, this preparation for the coming crucifixion seems perfectly appropriate. But it was the last thing Peter wanted to hear, and he started exercising his newfound authority by rebuking Jesus: "God forbid it, Lord! This shall never happen to You." Rather than expressing appreciation for his concern, Jesus surprised Peter by sharply replying, "Get behind Me, Satan!" (Matthew 16:22-23).

"Get behind Me, Satan!" seems like a severe response to a man who momentarily lost sight of the Kingdom and forgot Who he was rebuking. Peter just wanted to stop this insane journey towards death.

Who can blame Peter? From the moment Jesus said to Peter and his brother, "Follow Me. I will make you fishers of men," they saw the dead raised from the grave, thousands fed from a single lunch sack, demons cast out, the blind regain sight, and the deaf hear. Jesus taught and preached with more authority than anyone Peter had ever heard. Huge crowds adored Jesus, and Peter was His right-hand man. Peter had even walked on water and would one day have the keys to the kingdom of heaven! Life was good, and to lose the good times would be a catastrophe.

The strength of Jesus' rebuke indicates Peter's attempt to dissuade Jesus from the cross was extremely dangerous. It was dangerous for at least three reasons. First, taking on the sins of the world was hard enough without your friends trying to discourage you. Second, Peter's attempt to protect Jesus, instead of follow Him, placed Peter at a level where it is easy to lose sight of submission, service, love, mercy, and forgiveness.

Perhaps the most extreme example of this today is a controversial so-called church that proclaims "God Hates Fags" on its website. While Peter's rebuke of Jesus was far from the hate speech of this disturbing group, positioning ourselves as God's self-appointed protectors endangers our witness.

The third reason Peter's attitude was dangerous was because of his motivation. Have you ever been on vacation and desperately wished you didn't have to go back to the real world? On the other hand, perhaps you love your job, hobby, or habit and would never dream of giving it up for anybody or anything. Either extreme is, like Peter's attitude, a form of self-centered covetousness which, when followed, can cause us to miss God's will for our lives entirely.

Peter was on a dangerous path which only leads to failure:

You are a stumbling block to Me; for you are not setting your mind on God's interests, but man's. If anyone wishes to come after Me, he must deny himself, and take up his cross and follow Me. For whoever wishes to save his life will lose it; but whoever loses his life for My sake will find it. For what will it profit a man if he gains the whole world and forfeits his soul? Or what will a man give in exchange for his soul? (Matthew 16:23-26)

Peter went from being the man with the keys to the Kingdom to being "Satan." The *rock* became a *stumbling block*. To say he was confused is an understatement. Failure frequently causes us, like Peter, to question or even lose our identity.

As if this wasn't bad enough, it is hard to imagine how much more intense this sense of failure became days later when Peter denied he knew Jesus while Jesus was on trial. Peter had even recently promised Jesus "if I have to die with You, I will not deny You" (Matthew 26:35). Peter's pride in his position of leadership must have been thoroughly shattered with nothing to replace it except an embarrassing realization he had completely failed Jesus.
Peter had gone all in for Jesus, and it had turned into a nightmare. Walking away and not looking back was probably a real temptation for Peter. Mason Cooley once said, "If you call failures experiments, you can put them in your resume and claim them as achievements." At this point in Peter's life, he would have had to write off the whole Jesus experience as just another experiment if he wanted to salvage any pride whatsoever.

Peter, James, and John weren't the only disciples to fail Jesus. It is hard to even imagine the loss and sorrow Jesus must have felt when He said it would have been better if His trusted disciple Judas had never been born (see Matthew 26:24).

The ancient Greeks and Romans created gods who understood human sin because they were sinful themselves. Zeus and his heavenly cohorts were constantly getting drunk, having illicit sex, and killing people for the thrill. The Bible's God has no such weaknesses. He is almighty and perfect. How is He supposed to really understand what I am going through unless He somehow experiences it Himself?

"For we do not have a high priest who cannot sympathize with our weaknesses, but One who has been tempted in all things as we are, yet without sin" (Hebrews 4:15).

The phrase "One who has been tempted" in this Hebrews passage brings a new meaning to the wilderness experience of Jesus. He went through the starvation and exhaustion of the wilderness, not to prove how strong He was, but so He could experience our weakness and the strength of our temptations.

I have only known one person who has ever voluntarily fasted from food as long as Jesus did. He was a preacher who fasted during a forty-day prayer emphasis for his church. On the forty-first day, he ended up in the hospital close to death. Fasting that long makes anyone weak and susceptible to temptation, especially when the tempter is saying "Turn these rocks into bread" and you, in fact, have the ability to do so.

In the history of the universe, God has only known weakness for the duration of one brief life. In the course of that life, He was never weaker and closer to the pain of humanity than in the wilderness and upon the cross.

When someone is truly hurting and there is nothing you can say that can make it any better, there is a powerful ministry of simply being present. Sitting with a person, putting your arm around them, holding their hand, or just quietly sharing the pain of being human is sometimes the best we can do.

It is Jesus' experience of the pain of humanity—our weakness, the power of temptation, and the frustration of failure—that leads us to Paul's conclusion, "let us draw near with confidence to the throne of grace, so that we may receive mercy and find grace to help in time of need" (Hebrews 4:16). We often flee from Jesus because of failure's shame when He wants most to draw near and embrace us in His love's compassion. Even when we don't know what to say to God, there is healing just sitting in His presence.

Because of Jesus' experiences in the wilderness, with His disciples, and upon the cross, we know God understands and wants to help us when we fail. All He is asking is that we genuinely, humbly seek Him. When we seek Him, we find His throne is a throne of grace. At the same time, we must remember what Peter learned. The throne of grace is still a throne. He is and must be in charge. As we try to make sense out of our failures, we must seek His perspective on our life and not impose our own will on Him.

Discovering God's perspective is especially important, because He may have plans we cannot fathom. While God wants to help us avoid and overcome failure, there is also a place for it in His kingdom. Failure is as prevalent as sin and yet is not sin. Sin is failure, but failure is not sin. Psalm 115:3 says, "But our God is in the heavens; He does whatever He pleases." If failure pleases God, then it is the best thing that could happen as God uses it to accomplish His will.

Just consider Jeremiah. In Jeremiah 7:27-28, God told Jeremiah, "You shall speak all these words to them, but they will not listen to you; and you shall call to them, but

17

they will not answer you. You shall say to them ..." God told him to proclaim His message, and yet He also promised this proclamation would fall on deaf ears.

This reminds me of when I was asked to start a church in a town in Utah that did not have any non-Mormon churches. I spent over six months going door-to-door and organizing block parties, trying unsuccessfully to reach one person or start one Bible study. I remember going down one block in a neighborhood where every house I visited received a phone call immediately after I arrived telling them not to talk to me. It is difficult when you have a message and no one will hear it. We finally moved the church plant to another community where people were more open to the gospel.

Can you imagine how difficult Jeremiah's lifetime of ministry was, knowing his success was only in his obedience, not in the results? No wonder he is called the weeping prophet. God gave him a revelation of judgment, and there was nothing he could do to stop the terrible things he was preaching about. What Jeremiah probably didn't know as he was struggling through each day of frustrating obedience was that God would preserve his writings and his ministry would inspire believers around the world for thousands of years.

We have one life to live, and no one wants to spend it in failure. If Jeremiah teaches us anything, it is that things will not always go the way we want them to. When we fail for whatever reason to achieve what we set out to accomplish in this broken world, we must trust in the sovereignty of God, believing God is bigger than our failure and can even make our failure work out to His glory. As Paul said in Romans 8:28, "we know that God causes all things to work together for good to those who love God, to those who are called according to His purpose." Because of this, whatever we are going through, we trust Jesus understands, and nothing we are going through has caught Him unprepared. You will never hear God say, "Oops! Didn't see that one coming."

Jeremiah wasn't the only person in the Bible who had to trust in God's ability to overcome his shortfalls. In 2 Corinthians 11, Paul was sharing about his struggles in ministry when he said, "If I have to boast, I will boast of what pertains to my weakness" (vs. 30). Later in the same book, Paul discusses a time when he plead with God to remove a personal area of weakness.

And He has said to me, "My grace is sufficient for you, for power is perfected in weakness." Most gladly, therefore, I will rather boast about my weaknesses, so that the power of Christ may dwell in me. (2 Corinthians 12:9)

Paul's simple statement "power is perfected in weakness" reveals one of the greatest problems with the Culture of Success. We spend countless hours trying to get rid of weaknesses. We go to school to strengthen our minds. We go to gyms and do aerobics in front of our television sets to get rid of physical weaknesses. We go to seminars and conferences to strengthen our performance at work. We go to church to strengthen our spirituality. We go to counselors to strengthen our relationships. While all of these attempts at self-improvement are fine, nothing will ever overcome all of our weaknesses or stop all our failures.

While weaknesses are something to be loathed, hidden, and overcome in the Culture of Success, the apostle Paul learned the hard way that weaknesses are not something to

19

be hated or embarrassed about. They are something to be owned and boasted about, because God can often receive the greatest glory through human weaknesses.

We have two foster sons from the Democratic Republic of the Congo. Even though they came to us as teenagers, they had never attended public school. In their home country, the closest school was too far away, and attending would require walking through rebel-held war zones. When they arrived in the United States they spoke about five words of English. While they were provided some rudimentary education in reading and math in a Kenyan refugee camp, their first year with us was their first full year in public school.

Even though they had virtually no formal education, they started school in standard ninth-grade classes. Talk about weakness. Talk about being set up for failure. The fact that they finished the year on the honor roll is a testimony to the amazing support they received when arriving at their school. Their story would not be as significant or impressive if you swept their lack of schooling under the rug in shame.

Unfortunately, that is exactly what we do with our weaknesses and our resulting failures. Somehow, we feel we are being a better representative of God if no one knows we have a problem or that we have failed. The exact opposite is the truth.

Obviously, we all have our areas of weakness we find embarrassing. I, for one, am terrible at basketball. I have always been terrible at basketball. As a young child, I spent a lot of time trying to figure out how to get that ball through the hoop. I remember standing in the school gym practicing dribbling and having other kids laugh at me.

When kids chose teams, I wasn't the last one chosen. I was usually not chosen at all. It eventually became clear I would never be a basketball player, and I pursued other sports.

Michael Jordan—possibly the greatest basketball player of all time—made a movie called *Space Jam* in which the basketball skills of NBA players were transferred to cartoon characters via a magic basketball. If I could get my hands on that magic basketball and somehow absorb Michael Jordan's skills, I might suddenly play well. On the other hand, the glory for my play would not be my own. It would belong to the one who paid the price of long, hard hours of practice. My newly found success would require honest praise for Michael Jordan if I wanted to be anything more than a fake and a fraud.

When we boast in our weaknesses and are honest about our failures, we open the door for the power of Christ to rest on us and focus other people's attention on the transformation and empowerment of God. God is then able to receive the glory and not us.

One of the most popular stories in the Bible is the story of Jonah. Jonah was a prophet who was chosen by God to preach to the ancient city of Nineveh, the capital of the Assyrian empire, a huge city in what today is northern Iraq. It was also immersed in the worship of Ishtar with its sacred prostitution. While God declared Nineveh to be an evil place, it is also where God sent Jonah to preach.

Jonah was so excited about the calling, he immediately went the opposite direction and got on a ship to get as far away from Nineveh as possible. Talk about failure to do God's will. It took a huge storm and a giant fish to get Jonah back on track. What catches my attention most about

Jonah is not the giant fish or his eventual obedience but Jonah's testimony after he delivered his message.

I don't know if God used Jonah's horrendous appearance after spending time in the belly of the fish or if God used the power of Jonah's message. Whatever God used, Jonah's ministry was successful. Amazingly successful. The people of Nineveh repented, and God spared the city. Jonah was elated ... or was he?

But it greatly displeased Jonah and he became angry. He prayed to the Lord and said, "Please Lord, was not this what I said while I was still in my own country? Therefore ... O Lord, please take my life from me, for death is better to me than life." (Jonah 4:1-3)

In his success, Jonah was so angry and frustrated he wanted to die.

My question is, how do we know any of this happened? How do we know Jonah initially ran away from God's call, only being forced into the Nineveh ministry by *extreme* measures? How do we know Jonah was small-minded and would rather see Nineveh destroyed than see the people repent and be spared? How do we know Jonah was suicidal and angry with God?

The only source for any of this information would have been Jonah himself. If Jonah had lived in the Culture of Success, the book of Jonah may have been much shorter.

The Book of Jonah

Chapter One

Jonah was called by God to preach to Nineveh. Jonah didn't want to go at first but eventually obeyed. Jonah preached for several days and a great revival of repentance broke out in Nineveh, leading God to spare the city from destruction. Jonah went home.

End of Book

The fact that the Bible is honest about the ugliness of Jonah's failures is testimony to the fact that Jonah saw his own miserable attitude and grew to understand God's love for all mankind. Had he not, the book of Jonah, as it currently exists, could not have been written. On the other hand, because he did, *all* the glory in the story goes to God.

The same thing could be said about Moses' failures and Peter's failures. Moses angered God twice so severely God was ready to kill Moses the first time, and God banned Moses from entering the Promised Land the second time. The only reason we know about these failures is because Moses wrote the book of Exodus. In addition, Peter was undoubtedly the only witness to both painful interchanges between himself and Jesus.

The Ministry of Failure allowed each of these men to testify how their worst failures were changed by the grace of God to reveal the glory of God. Through countless stories like theirs and through the life of Jesus, we see clearly that God understands and wants to redeem our failures in His ongoing, loving story of grace. When He does, it will then be our privilege to share our own testimony of what He, and He alone, has done.

Michelle Morningstar's Story

I was at a party when a young sailor caught my eye. It was clear he felt the same attraction. Unfortunately, we were both in relationships. When those relationships fell apart, we began dating. After a lightning-quick romance, we were engaged March 23, 1999. I knew he was the one for me when he stopped in traffic to visit a small rose stand on the highway—just because he wanted to see me smile. I knew then he would move heaven and earth for me. After he returned from a six-month deployment, we were married on January 22, 2000.

After a brief honeymoon, we settled into our roles as a military couple. We decided early on we wanted to start a family and, without hesitation, we embarked on that journey, not knowing how difficult that journey would be.
Over six years, I had five micro-miscarriages, all before there was even a heartbeat. My first miscarriage was on my twentieth birthday. The doctor treating me said I suffered from dysfunctional uterine bleeding. Unfortunately. he did not know what caused it or how to treat it.

Over the next few years, I can remember being curled up in bed screaming from the pain, despondent, begging God and anyone who was listening to please stop the pain. I had a slew of surgeries to try to correct the problem. I also had to take powerful medication to treat a disease that had no cause and, thus, no cure … and which made me feel like I was crazy.

Eventually, doctors told me they thought the problem was "all in my head." Doctors and therapists alike tried to make me believe I was crazy at best and a hypochondriac at worst. I was miserable, homesick, and in pain all the time.

My young husband spent so much time at the hospital with me they should have rented us out a room.

I became inconsolable and angry. I was angry at my husband. I was angry at the doctors. I was angry at myself, and I was angry at God. I begged God to give me what I desperately wanted, and I caused countless fights and arguments with my young and scared husband who was just as lost as I was. I thought about divorcing my husband so he wouldn't have to deal with a broken wife.

Family and friends were having one, two, and more children, and when I went to a birthday party or a welcome baby party, I was of course happy and delighted for the new parent-to-be, but I was silently screaming inside. Jealousy and despair are very tricky friends, and I suffered from both. I eventually stopped receiving invitations to those parties as family members decided my issues were too difficult to deal with.

While I still tried to pray, I felt like it was God's fault my body had betrayed me. I left my church and withdrew into a shell of myself, determined to live out my life miserable and angry at the world as they had something I wanted and couldn't have. Like a child, I pouted and screamed, and threw the biggest, longest temper tantrum ever.

Our lives became a sea of tests, procedures, medications, and science in a quest that seemingly had no end in sight. We were losing ourselves in the process. All I ever wanted was to be a mother and have a child and live happily ever after, but that seemed like a dream out of my grasp. I was finally diagnosed with stage-three endometriosis and began taking a drug called Lupron. Unfortunately, the drug only made my condition worse. Even after being diagnosed and trying a variety of infertility alternatives, we were unsuccessful and finally consigned ourselves to not having children. God's will be done.

It was then we discovered a procedure called embryo adoption. I frantically started making phone calls and putting in applications and doing phone interviews. For the first time in a long time, I could feel the hand of God guiding me. He guided the words from my husband's mouth to my waiting, eager ears, that we should look into this more. He guided my shaking hands as I dialed the number of the cryo-bank and talked to the receptionist to be put on their waiting list. We were told it would be an eighteen-month wait, but in just three months we were ready to move forward.

We picked out embryos who were frozen in 1994 but were, as my doctor told us, "perfect." We were filled with sheer joy when we glimpsed them in the tube and felt exhausted exhilaration as we selected two to be implanted.

I have written an e-book called, *She Grew in My Heart*, where I share my story in more detail. In this e-book, I describe this time:

We called the clinic and arranged for the precious cargo to be transported to my doctor's office and picked a day for implantation. With this came a prescription for more high dose medications and preparation for pregnancy. These involved months of hormone preparations and with that, craziness ensued. I once got into a fight with my husband's friend over a slice of lemon meringue pie. I desperately wanted the pie and sent them out to get it, but when they got back, I didn't want it anymore.

One hundred and thirty-five ... that's the number of preparatory shots I took to get ready to be pregnant. Some were daily and some were weekly. The first of them was given to me on July 4, 2007 in a small bathroom in Inner Harbor, Baltimore, Maryland, by my mother-in-law. My husband had a joke that he was practicing for lawn darts when he had to give me my daily shots.

I believe God was there in that room the day the miracle of implantation was performed, and it is only through His grace my precious child is here today.

Toward the end of my pregnancy, I ended up in the hospital again as my body once again tried to betray us, but God had me and my child in His hands. On March 23, 2009, my beautiful daughter made her entrance into this world.

I wish I could say since the birth of our child everything has been wonderful. We have, however, seen our fair share of trouble and the spirit of despair I suffered with for so long began to wash over me again.

Fortunately, I have been blessed with a wonderful pastor. I went to him to gain perspective and because I was feeling guilty about my anger with God. His response was something to the effect of "God is big enough to handle it." I was floored. In all my lessons from childhood on, I was taught we should be respectful, fearful, and revere our heavenly Father. It was certainly not okay to be angry at Him. Here was someone telling me I was allowed to be angry at my Creator. He told me God wouldn't love me any less, and I wasn't a heathen for feeling human emotions and anger. God created me with these feelings, and it was okay for me to express them as they were part of being human, and being human was okay.

Suddenly, a revelation hit me. I wasn't going to hell because I went through a "spiritual crisis." God and I might have been estranged, but I had never truly been apart from Him. He had heard my cries, my pleas, my prayers, and He had answered in His time. I had made it through because my Creator had been there all along.

He was with me in the comforting eyes and loving arms of my husband. He was with me in the friends and family who let me rage and scream and cry and then picked me back up again. He was with me in the whisper of faith and hope and tenacity and stubbornness which kept us searching for another way. He was listening all the time, and He was there the night my baby was born, ushering me into a new path of parenthood—showing me the meaning of His perfect love. Because of His love, I know my physical problems do not mean I am broken; I am just put together in an alternate way. He is still there, and He is still listening and loving me.

Meditation Moment

- What episodes from your life story would you never dream of putting on a resume? Are there any ways in which you have been better prepared for life through these experiences?

- Do you believe Jesus Christ knew the pain of failure? If so, what does that mean for your life?

- Failure is frequently accompanied with a host of emotions. What lessons can we learn from Michelle Morningstar's story about handling the anger, frustration, and guilt of failure?

- If you wrote purpose statements for your professional life, spiritual life, entertainment life, and family life, what would they be? Do any of these purpose statements conflict with each other? If they conflict, which is your priority?

- In the United States, we believe in the separation of church and state. Many people also believe in separating their spiritual life from other areas of their lives, especially their failures. The Bible, however, tells us God is Creator of everything. As our Creator, He claims lordship over every area of our existence. If this is true, what does that mean about your life? What does it mean about your failures?

- Is it possible God has been working behind the scenes to bring about failures in your life? Would He ever do that? If so, why and what would it mean to you?

- Do you have a testimony of how God has taken one of your failures and transformed it for good? If so, have you ever shared it with someone else?

Chapter Three

Grace, Law and Failure

Surely our griefs He Himself bore,
And our sorrows He carried.
Isaiah 53:4

Niko Hulslander's powerlifting career lasted over twenty years. From the very beginning, he showed tremendous promise. His first bench press contest was in March of 1994. He came in third with a bench of 415 pounds. As a young lifter, he won the junior world title for lifters, age nineteen through twenty-two, beating a record formerly held by Mark Henry, a famous Olympic lifter and professional wrestler.

When Niko lifted, he brought an unusual level of intensity and drama. In 2006, Robert Keller, one of our nation's top weightlifting referees, described Hulslander as "the spirit and heart of USA Powerlifting." That was the same year Niko lifted 2133 pounds combined between the squat, bench press, and dead lift. An impressive amount indeed.

Niko's career ended right after he went to South Africa for the world championships, where he was ranked number one in the world. He wasn't able to compete because he tore his lateral quad a couple days before the meet. But the injury was not what ended his career. Niko had an emotional meltdown which led him to leave the sport of weightlifting.

Niko's problems stemmed from a condition called "performance orientation." He was addicted to the praise and affirmation his sport and professional life gave him. His life, his passion, and his identity were all found in the gym he ran and his weightlifting career. While he was married and had children, he funneled so much of his money back into his gym, his family suffered. Seventy and eighty-hour work weeks took him almost entirely out of his family's life, even when his six-year-old child was diagnosed with type 1 diabetes. The final straw, however, was an emotional affair at the gym which he finally had to confess to his pastor and his wife.

It felt like hell. I thought I lost everything. I was depressed. I remember lying in bed with the covers up over me. If I am not working, I am not a man. If I am not providing for my family, I am not a man. If I am not lifting the way I should be lifting, I am not a man. If I am not winning trophies, I am not a man. If I don't have a relationship with my wife, I am not a man.

It was either go get some help or continue down the path of destruction. I was tired. I was physically, emotionally, spiritually just drained. I was exhausted. Fortunately, I was able to get some inpatient counseling. I found out what "performance orientation" is all about. How as a man if you feel like your dignity is stripped away, if your functionality isn't what society thinks it should be, you can really get tripped up. That was 2014. I haven't competed since.

I went for about a year after that being unemployed. I applied for seventy-one jobs, and I got seventy-one rejections. I got some work here and there. A young man I used to train with was leaving his job, and he called me up and asked if I was still looking for something. I was like, "Yeah, I will take anything." I drove around and collected quarters from air machines where you pump up your tires at the gas station. I had a huge territory of 560 of those machines. Something totally out of my world and what I used to be involved with—on my knees every day collecting quarters.

Driving around allowed me to listen to some wonderful preachers on the radio. I was drawn to James McDonald. He has an in-your-face coaching aspect to his messages. He also uses a term I like: "I am that man." That is what I try to share with other men who come to me and say, "Niko, I am embarrassed. I am depressed. I am angry. I am struggling with this. I am struggling with that. I use alternatives to make myself happy, whether it is drugs, alcohol, or pornography." I just look at them and say, "I am that man. You are not alone."

Niko was eventually restored by God and is now running a non-profit gym ministry. His lesson, "I am that man" serves all of us well.

There is a human condition of failure which makes us all "that man."

Every person who has ever existed has had a missing-the-mark problem. The Greek word for missing the mark is *hamartia*. It was used in ancient writing to refer to the point when someone does something causing the story to take a turn for the worse. In English, it is translated *sin*. "For all have sinned and come short of the glory of God" (Romans 3:23).

From a Christian perspective, *the glory of God* is the ultimate definition of the best life possible. It is living life so perfectly that people see God in everything we do. It is the standard of right and wrong no one, except Jesus, has ever lived up to. "Do my actions or lack of actions in some way glorify God?" is the question that must be asked to determine if we have missed the mark and failed morally.

Mankind first became aware of how acute our failure was through the ministry of Moses. God gave Moses a collection of rules, standards, and expectations which were intended to reveal God's will to the nation of Israel. These rules, standards, and expectations were called the Law. Moses' revelation of the Law began with the Ten Commandments and continued until it became a complicated system of behavior impacting every aspect of life from diet to property ownership to worship.

The Culture of Success views this Law as a way of standing apart from the rest of mankind. In this tradition, following rules and regulations becomes a way of currying favor with God and earning entry into heaven. One person becomes better than another because he obeys more of the law than his neighbor.

The purpose of the Law was never to instill us with pride over our goodness. Paul tells us in I Timothy 1:9 that the law was not made for the righteous but was instead given for "those who are lawless and rebellious, for the ungodly and sinners." During WWII, our government came out with a series of public service posters featuring slogans like "Loose lips sink ships" and "He's watching you!" Just as these slogans were written for people who tended to talk too much, the law was intended for sinners who failed to keep it.

The law is God's revelation of what we ought to do. It is moral and right. It is also a revelation of what we do not do. Sinners, by definition, are not perfect, and no amount of good deeds can change the fact we have failed. Rather than somehow making us perfect, the law was written to lead us to the Ministry of Failure. Just consider the first commandments of the law as found in Exodus 20:3-17.

1. You shall have no other gods before me.
2. You shall not make for yourself an idol.
3. You shall not take the name of the Lord your God in vain.
4. Remember the sabbath day, to keep it holy.
5. Honor your father and your mother.
6. You shall not murder.
7. You shall not commit adultery.
8. You shall not steal.
9. You shall not bear false witness against your neighbor.
10. You shall not covet.

How far down through these commandments do you get before finding one you stumble over? I don't even make it through the first one. And I am not alone. There once was a man who asked Jesus, "what good thing shall I do, that I may have eternal life?" (Matthew 19:16). Jesus pointed this young man to these commandments.

When the man claimed to have obeyed the commandments fully, Jesus pointed him to the Ministry of Failure.

The young man said, "All these things I have kept; what am I still lacking?" Jesus said to him, "If you wish to be complete, go and sell your possessions and give to the poor, and you will have treasure in heaven; and come, follow Me." But when the young man heard this statement, he went away grieving; for he was one who owned much property. (Matthew 19:20-22)

Rather than encouraging the man for his good behavior, Jesus made sure he stumbled over his idol. The man had placed money before God in his heart. Unfortunately, his failure drove the young man away from God instead of to Him. The purpose of the Law is to reveal our failures and draw us into the arms of God and His loving forgiveness. This is the Ministry of Failure. "Through the law comes the knowledge of sin" (Romans 2:19-20).

"Therefore, the Law has become our tutor to lead us to Christ, so that we may be justified by faith" (Galatians 3:24).

The reality of our sin reminds me of an incident in my high school. One of my science teachers sought to enforce control over her classes by screaming at any child with whom she was unhappy. Needless to say, she was not very popular. One day, this teacher had to step out of class for a minute. Some of her students asked another student to watch the door for her return. While their guard stood sentry, the students slipped some bacteria they were studying into the teacher's coffee. Later that day, the teacher became violently sick and was sent to the local hospital where her stomach was pumped.

I was the student chosen to watch out for the teacher's return. At the time, I did not know why I was watching out for her and did not learn about what the other students had done until the next day when our teacher did not return to school. The moment I learned of the horrible thing that was done to her, I was morally obligated to let someone know. The boys could have killed the teacher, and there should have been consequences for poisoning her. I did not say anything at the time because I was afraid of what the other students would say about me.

God does not have the luxury of pretending sin does not exist and does not need to be punished. Sin separates us from God and prevents us from fulfilling our purpose, to love God and glorify Him forever. Sin is a rejection of love, the ultimate good. It therefore demands the ultimate punishment: "the wages of sin is death" (Romans 6:23).

God would be perfectly justified to let mankind die and spend eternity separated from Him. We deserve it. If He had turned His back on us when we turned our backs on Him, can you imagine what our world would be like? If Jesus had never come? If there was no Bible? If there was no hope? We don't have to look far. The holocaust of Nazism, the terrors of the Soviet gulag, Castro's political prisons, and North Korea's policies of starvation and torture are all testimony to the quality of societies without God.

A John Lennon hit song, "Imagine," once asked us to imagine the impossible—no heaven, no hell, only sky and people who only live for today. Lennon's song asks us to imagine the impossible, because you can't have both. You can't have everyone living selfishly and not have hell. History is proof. Whenever mankind lives for today with no divine influence, life becomes hellish.

God's love demanded another solution: a way sin's horrible punishment could be paid, and yet a relationship with mankind could be assured. That is the reason Jesus came. "God demonstrates His own love toward us, in that while we were yet sinners, Christ died for us" (Romans 5:8). The Bible calls Jesus at this point of truth a "stumbling stone" because many people struggle with Jesus being the solution.

My wife's brother was a brilliant man who stumbled over Jesus because he doubted the trustworthiness of the Bible. We were talking once and I showed him some Old Testament prophesies about Jesus. My brother-in-law, who usually loved to debate, was speechless. He simply responded, "That's impressive." Judaism and Christianity are the only two religions in the world built on the solid foundation of prophesy.

One of the most amazing of these Old Testament prophesies was written 700 years before Jesus came and yet tells us clearly in Isaiah 53:4-6 why He would come:

Surely our griefs He Himself bore,
And our sorrows He carried;
Yet we ourselves esteemed Him stricken,
Smitten of God, and afflicted.
But He was pierced through for our transgressions,
He was crushed for our iniquities;

37

The chastening for our well-being fell upon Him,
And by His scourging we are healed.
All of us like sheep have gone astray,
Each of us has turned to his own way;
But the Lord has caused the iniquity of us all
To fall on Him.

Transgressions and iniquity are just other words for sin.
If Isaiah was correct and Jesus died for our sins, what do
we do? That depends on whether we are living in the
Culture of Success or experiencing the Ministry of Failure.
Paul said our salvation has nothing to do with our ability to
fulfill God's law.

But now apart from the Law the righteousness of God has
been manifested ... for all have sinned and fall short of the
glory of God, being justified as a gift by His grace through
the redemption which is in Christ Jesus. (Romans 3:21-24)

I love the phrase "as a gift by His grace" in these verses.
We find this gift again in Ephesians 2:8-9: "For by grace
you have been saved through faith; and that not of
yourselves, it is the gift of God; not as a result of works, so
that no one may boast." Gifts are always paid for by
someone else. The only boasting the receiver of a gift can
make is in their need for the gift and in the generosity of
the giver.

Many years ago, I met an extraordinary man. He was a lifelong missionary to an Indian tribe appointed by his church.
He and his wife were nice enough to let me stay in their
house while I was in town for my uncle's funeral. The night
before the funeral, I stayed up late talking to my host. He
had recently retired and told me he only had one regret

from his years of ministry. He regretted never becoming a Christian himself. After recovering from my shock, I had the privilege of telling him about the free gift of salvation. Unfortunately, he had a hard time believing salvation could be as simple as trusting God's truth.

While we might want to *pay* God for our salvation by obeying the law and being a good person, righteousness is experienced totally apart from the rules and regulations of the law. Righteousness comes as a gift from God through a faith relationship with Jesus Christ. This gift was paid for by Jesus upon His cross and is a testimony to the love of our heavenly Father, not our moral earning potential in the heavenly kingdom. As a result, salvation must be accepted in a simple prayer of faith and lived out in humble thankfulness and love.

My life, for one, was radically changed when someone asked me if I had made a personal covenant with God by accepting what Jesus had done for me. I lied to the man and told him I had. I then went home, got on my knees, and cried out, "God, I believe!" The next day I told my cousin I had changed and he told me not to worry—salvation was like the flu, I would get over it. I have had the *flu* for thirty-seven years. Must be some kind of record.

While salvation is a wonderful gift, it is just the beginning of a life with God. When Christians live in a religious version of the Culture of Success, they miss an important truth. "No one is justified by the Law before God ... the righteous man shall live by faith" (Galatians 3:11).

Righteousness is always free, before salvation and after. Every act of devotion, every ministry, every testimony we give is built on and motivated by gratefulness for a goodness we don't deserve and can't earn.

I was sitting in the back of a bus when a rough group of young, loud men got on. They came back and sat all around me. We had a great time together as we talked about God's plan for their lives and Jesus' gift of salvation. While I enjoyed our conversation, none of them seemed interested in learning more. I got off the bus when it reached my stop and was shocked when a woman leaped off the bus and chased me down. She had heard our conversation and wanted to know more. It wasn't even her stop.

When we live in the daily reality of God's grace, the spiritual hunger and humility which drives someone to leap off a bus to learn about Jesus doesn't stop with salvation. It simply changes into our driving motivation to live in joyful service. "As you have received Christ Jesus the Lord, so walk in Him" (Colossians 2:6). True ministry is a natural overflow from a grateful and blessed heart, not a duty.

Another consequence of this gift of righteousness is that our failures do not need to define who we are. Romans 11:29 says, "the gifts and the calling of God are irrevocable." God does not regret His relationship with us when He sees us fail. After all, His love came to us "while we were yet sinners" (Romans 5:8).

When we were engaged, my wife and I went on a double date with her parents. After eating shark for the first and only time in her life, my future wife came down with a horrible case of food poisoning. I stayed up with her through most of the night as she threw up repeatedly. By morning she knew beyond a shadow of a doubt I was committed to her, because I had seen her at her worst and yet—when she saw the way I looked at her—she knew I still loved her. I appreciate how she felt because that is very similar to how I know God loves me. He has seen me at my worst and still loves me.

At the same time, I would have been one horrible fiancée if I had not wanted my wife to experience a better life than food poisoning gave her. While God loves me, He also does not want me to live in the pain of moral failure. Unfortunately, getting cleaned up is not always easy. Addressing moral failure is often messy. This is because it always starts in the reality of painful truth. The Psalmist captures this pain in Psalm 44:15. "All day long my dishonor is before me, and my humiliation has overwhelmed me."

Two of our closest friends were overwhelmed with this sense of dishonor and humiliation one night as they sat on our couch pouring out their hearts and hurt over a devastating moral failure that threatened their marriage. My wife and I listened, prayed, and struggled to find the right words to help them make it through the night. That night began a long journey of seeking God, pain, anger, distrust, confession, accountability, and gradual healing. Today, our friends' marriage is stronger than ever and God has used their failure to equip them as counselors in Whatever It Takes (WIT) Ministries.

WIT Ministries is a ministry of Paul and Jenny Speed. Their WIT Marriage Intensive weekend is a retreat unlike any I have ever experienced. It is not for couples looking to rekindle a smoldering spark. It is for couples who don't even have a spark—couples whose marriage has been devastated by things such as extra-marital affairs, pornography, masturbation, prostitution, homosexuality, and abandonment. The success of the program is its biblical foundation and its demand that attendees be willing to do whatever it takes to heal their marriage.

Paul and Jenny Speed are not the first people to ask us to do whatever it takes to overcome failure. Jesus Himself said, "If your right eye makes you stumble, tear it out and throw it from you; for it is better for you to lose one of the parts of your body, than for your whole body to be thrown into hell" (Matthew 5:29). Obviously, Jesus is not calling us to self-mutilate. He is telling us to determine the causes of our moral failures and do whatever it takes get rid of them.

In the Culture of Success, you use religion to hide your sins. You attend church. If Sunday services are entertaining, you may even learn to like it and try to get involved. You clean up your act. You learn to talk the talk. When you sin, you confess it to God, but you would never dream of confessing it to anyone else. Who knows what they would say about you?

When you experience the Ministry of Failure, the pain of your failure hits you like a ton of bricks. You see your sin for what it is, the reason for Jesus' death and your own spiritual emptiness. Your moral failure drives you to the cross where you gladly and humbly pray, accepting the grace of God through the death of Jesus. You then do whatever it takes to remove the causes of your failure and renew your relationship with God and with people you have hurt.

Jesus once said, "Everyone who hears these words of Mine and acts on them may be compared to a wise man who built his house on the rock. And the rain fell, and the floods came, and the winds blew and slammed against that house; and yet it did not fall, for it had been founded on the rock" (Matthew 7:24-25).

When you do whatever it takes to build your life on the solid rock of God's truth, no one can promise you the floods and winds won't still come. Life will always have storms. A whatever-it-takes attitude is the difference between a life that crumbles and one that will stand the test of eternity.

For Niko Huslander *whatever it takes* involved confession of sin, walking away from his career, enrolling in inpatient counseling, finding the support of accountability partners, ongoing counseling with his wife, removing social media from his life, time restrictions at work, open and honest communication with his wife (no matter how difficult), using "re-directive words" when he feels triggered and, most of all, renewing his commitment to Jesus Christ every single day.

> *When I finally returned to the gym, I was glad I went through what I went through. God gave me an opportunity to break down in order to be able to surrender. I was built back up in order to understand I need Him every minute of every day and to see I don't have to perform to be loved. I don't need*

people's affirmation, and I don't have to live in my past. I can learn from my past, but I don't have to live there. Yes, it hurts and recovery is a process of forgiving and asking for forgiveness.

Early in my weightlifting career, I showed my coach Dave Schleich a certificate I had earned for setting a world record. He said, "So, doesn't mean anything to me. Doesn't mean anything to those people out there on that sidewalk. You don't know how strong you could be." Now I know strength doesn't just mean how strong you are physically under the barbell. Real strength is emotional, mental, spiritual, and relational strength with family and friends.

Niko found a better life because he was willing to face his sins and pursue God. But what if you don't believe in sin? In 2013, George Elerick wrote a blog for the Huffington Post website titled, *Sin Does Not Exist*. In order to argue the point, he reduces the world to a single individual and says, "If we were the only one alive in the world—we would not need the definition [of evil], hence evil emerges in a communal setting." In other words, evil is an invention of society and not a spiritual reality. The weakness to his argument is his argument itself. His argument is an admission that, when you get two people in a relationship, the possibility of evil exists.

I struggled with the reality of evil many years ago when a one-time visitor to our church wrote asking me to visit her. I drove four hours across Pennsylvania and waited for a couple more hours to see her because she forgot to put me on her visitation list. We talked a long time before she finally told me why she was in jail. She gave her young daughters sexually to her boyfriend in order to ensure he stayed with her. It was more than I could handle. I know there is a limit to my ability to accept and love, because I reached my limit that day. I babbled something about getting a local pastor to visit her, and I left.

While I was unable to look at this woman's evil and love her anyway, I thank God His love doesn't fail. If it did, this failed mother would not be the only one without hope. I would be lost. "I am that man!" Evil exists because of my moral failure, and I have no right to judge anyone, including her. Judgment is God's domain ... but so is unconditional love. Through the horrors of Jesus' death, God has perfectly balanced love and justice. He became "that man" so we might have hope. If God balked because we have failed Him horribly, the cross would never have happened. The greatest mystery is not the existence of evil. It is that God offers each of us, no matter how badly we have failed, the miracle of grace, forgiveness, restoration, and salvation.

God's grace is a great story to tell, and our failures are an ever-present backdrop for His story.

Beckie's Story

In the spring of 1830, the Mormon Church was established and within twelve years both sides of my family had joined. They were part of the early immigration that traveled across the plains as Mormon pioneers and helped to settle the Utah territory. My great-great-great grandfather was John D. Lee, the only person executed for his participation in the infamous Mountain Meadows Massacre. As you can see, my roots go deep in the Mormon Church. It has always been a large part of my identity.

I was raised in Clearfield, Utah, by parents who were always very active in the Mormon Church. My father was the bishop of our local ward for most of my childhood years, and my mother was always very active with her church callings. As I think back on my childhood, just about every memory is somehow related to the Mormon Church. Being Mormon was a lifestyle. One of my first memories was being stood on the pew during fast and testimony meeting when I was only three or four years old so I could testify that I knew the church was true, Joseph Smith was a prophet, and that I was thankful for the current prophet.

Growing up in Clearfield during the 60s and 70s and being a member of the only true church was wonderful. Everyone I knew was Mormon, and I really thought the rest of the world was too. I knew I must have been a very valiant spirit in my pre-existence to be able to be blessed by being born when Christ's church had been restored and into an active Mormon family who were sealed together not just for time but for all eternity too. I was proud of who I was and the future that lay ahead of me.

I was happy and outgoing, busily involved in church, with my job, in high school, and with my social life. I knew who I was and what I was, and I was excited about accomplishing all the goals I had set for my life.

When I was a senior in high school, something happened which would change the direction of my life forever. I met a boy, Gary, and thought he was the person I wanted to spend the rest of my life and all eternity with. We became engaged and just knew we would live happily ever after. We spent a lot of time together, and as we became more and more familiar with each other, the inevitable finally happened … we had sex one time. I knew it was wrong and that we had committed a very serious sin.

It didn't take long to realize I wasn't ready to get married and, even if I was, Gary wasn't the right person for me, so I ended the relationship.

A couple of months later I found out I was pregnant. I still remember the fear as I sat in the doctor's office listening to my options … adoption, getting married, or not getting married but keeping the baby. I knew the Mormon culture well enough to know that keeping the baby and not getting married was not an option. I also knew marrying Gary was not something I wanted, so the only other choice was adoption. I left the doctor's office that day and had to go home and tell my parents I had committed this serious sin and what had happened as a result of it.

When I came home it was decided it would be best if we kept everything a secret and didn't let anybody know what I had done. I had an uncle who lived in Salt Lake who accepted me and loved me in spite of the fact that I had committed this sin. He was not an active Mormon … in fact from a Mormon perspective he was a sinner. As I look at it now, I find it interesting he was the one who loved me when I had to hide from all the "religious" people I knew.

I spent the next few months living in Salt Lake with my Uncle Ken. He was so good to me and took wonderful care of me for the duration of the pregnancy.

47

In September of 1976, I gave birth to a healthy baby boy and then went through with the adoption process. I gave him up to a family who could give him the care he needed and which I was unable to give him. As I share this part of my testimony I want to make it perfectly clear that I believe the decision to give my son up was the best decision for him. Having said that, it was one of the hardest things I have ever had to do.

I came home after this experience and was expected to pick up and start my life again where I had left off. The only problem was I was a different person. My self-esteem was shattered. I was angry with God. Why did God allow me to get pregnant the one and only time I had sex? Why did that happen? Why did God put me through this? How was I going to go on and put it all behind me? What about my dreams for the future? How would I ever find a husband who would understand and love me even though I had sinned and been through the things that I had?

My brother gave me an autographed copy of a book, The Miracle of Forgiveness, written by the prophet of the church at the time, Pres. Spencer W. Kimball. This book said things I already knew. I had committed "the sin next to murder, your virtue is worth more than your life, and no unclean thing can enter the Kingdom of God." I knew the steps the Mormon Church taught us in order to achieve forgiveness very well.

Recognize I had done wrong
Abandon the sin
Repent
Serious sins like I committed needed to be discussed with the proper authorities
Restitution (if possible)
Never repeat the sin again

I followed the prescribed steps. I prayed and asked for forgiveness, and I also discussed my sin with my bishop and stake president. The only problem was I never felt forgiven. I felt like a fraud. I knew I was a sinner. I was different from all my Mormon friends. I wasn't one of them, and I knew I couldn't tell them what I had been through.

About a year later, I met a non-Mormon and married him. My husband loved and accepted me even though I had sinned, and he joined the Mormon Church about six months after we were married. We became active in our ward and looked forward to the time we could be sealed together forever. I was trying to live life like all of our Mormon friends and family, but deep down inside I knew I was a fraud.

Before we went to the temple, I repented to my bishop and stake president again but still never felt forgiven and cleansed of my sin. They told me I had been forgiven as far as the church was concerned, and I should just keep it secret and not ever talk about it again. (Every time I went in for another temple recommend or for an interview we would discuss it again … I was not forgiven and I knew it.) It never once crossed my mind that the problems I was having were because something was wrong with the Mormon Church and because I was trying to be perfect, which was impossible. I knew the Mormon Church was true, and it was me who had the problem.

I decided the only thing I could do was live the rest of my life with this huge skeleton in my closet. I knew I couldn't tell our friends or even my children what I had done or the results of it. I would look at our friends and wonder why they could be so perfect and I couldn't. I knew they would never accept me if they knew the truth about me, so I never told any of them what had happened. I lived my life as a fraud.

As a Mormon I was taught Jesus was perfect and that I could be too. What was wrong with me that I couldn't be perfect? I struggled because I knew the Mormon Church was true and my problems were a result of my sin. I was terrified of death because

I knew I was a sinner and there was no way I could ever make it to the Celestial Kingdom.

In May of 1996, we bought a new computer, and I was intrigued with the idea of communicating with people all over the world. I met a Mormon lady from Pennsylvania who had a group of friends she would chat with regularly on her computer, so I started visiting with them. In this group was a man, Derek Jones, who used the nickname EMT, because he was an emergency medical technician.

On June 13, 1996 our little neighbor girl, Amanda, came over crying because her eighteen-month-old cousin who lived down the street from us had wandered into the road and been hit by a car and killed the night before. I told Derek I had to shut down the computer so I could console Amanda.

The next day I told Derek what had happened and I also made the comment, "I hate death." Derek wanted to know why and my response was, "because I know I am not perfect and I will not go to the Celestial Kingdom when I die." Derek didn't know much about the teachings of Mormonism and didn't realize we were using the same words, but they had totally different meanings. He started sharing Scriptures with me and telling me I could pray to receive Christ. I didn't know what he was talking about, but I was sure he was wrong. The more we talked that evening, the more Derek could see this was not going to be an easy process.

I really wanted to teach Derek about Mormonism because I knew it was the only true church. I wanted to share with him how he could have an eternal family. Just because I was a sinner and would never make it to the Celestial Kingdom didn't stop me from thinking I owed it to others to share with them about Mormonism.

My discussions with Derek were such an eye-opener to me because I thought everyone believed the things I had been taught as facts. There was a pre-existence, Satan and Jesus were our spirit brothers, we had a heavenly Father and heavenly Mother who were the parents of our spirits, Jesus was the God of this world, heavenly Father, Jesus, and the Holy Ghost are all separate beings (one in purpose), the importance of the priesthood (the authority to act in God's name), heavenly Father and Jesus have bodies of flesh and bones, polygamy was something that God lived and even Jesus practiced when he was here on earth, certain sins couldn't be forgiven, and, most importantly, families could live together forever.

I really believed I could show Derek that Mormonism was the same church Jesus established when he was on the earth and that Joseph Smith restored the truths lost through the apostasy. All of these teachings were as real to me as gravity, the earth is round, and $2 + 2 = 4$.

When I found out Derek was an ordained minister, it didn't deter me at all. I remember my biggest concern about his role in his church was what title I was supposed to give him. He made me feel better when he told me most people just call him, "Boring."

We met on the computer regularly to discuss all of this. It seemed like every time we met, he would tell me of another person he had praying for me.

I would spend most nights with my Bible concordance and Mormon books getting a list of Scriptures, which would prove Mormonism was biblical. Time and time again, I was challenged to read the Scripture in context and found my proof Scriptures were not saying the things I had been taught they said. God was so merciful to me through this process, because at the same time the foundation of Mormonism was crumbling around my feet He was replacing it with Bible truths.

In April of 1997 I finally accepted the things God had been showing me through Derek's witness. I prayed to receive Christ as my Savior and asked Him to be the Lord of my life. By confessing my sins and accepting the forgiveness which was being offered so freely by Christ's sacrifice on the cross, I was finally relieved of the guilt I had carried for over twenty years.

It has taken time, but I have also come to be thankful for what God did through the guilt and pain I went through with the unwed pregnancy. God used it to help me to see my sinful condition. I needed to see perfection was not something I could achieve on my own. I needed to be humbled through all of this to be brought to the point of accepting Christ as my Lord and Savior and to see that salvation can only come through Him.

Whenever I read Romans 8:28 ("God causes all things to work together for good to those who love God"), I am reminded of how God used what I thought was the worst experience in my life to bring me to Him. It took over twenty-one years for me to see the reason all of this had to happen, but it is really a reminder to me that God is at work in our lives even at times when we think He has forgotten about us.

Meditation Moment

- Many people ask why God allows evil in the universe. If God is so good, why didn't He create the universe so evil could not exist? On the other hand, if evil wasn't at least possible, would good exist? If good and evil didn't exist in our universe, would it be possible for beings in this universe to truly know the God who is good?

- Take time to consider your life journey. What are the significant events that have brought you to where you are today? Can you see the hand of God in any of these events, even the failures?

- Have your failures ever overwhelmed you into a relationship with God through Jesus Christ? Have you ever considered the impact you could have on someone else by sharing the life lessons you have learned through these events?

- Do you have any broken relationships left behind in your life journey? What would you be willing to do to make these relationships whole again?

- Romans 5:10 says, "while we were [His] enemies we were reconciled to God through the death of His Son." What does this tell us about God's desire to make our relationship with Him whole again?

- What does it mean to you to say that our failures an ever-present backdrop to God's story of grace in our lives?

Chapter Four

Consequences

Consequences of failure are inevitable and usually beyond our control.

Chuck Colson is one of my lifetime heroes. When he died in 2012, every news article and obituary I read began with something like "Chuck Colson, disgraced, convicted Watergate conspirator ..." Even Christianity Today began his obituary with "The infamous convicted Nixon adviser."[2]

There was nothing Colson could do that would ever erase the legacy of his failure—a political break-in that brought down the president of the United States. Chuck Colson's involvement in Watergate led to his conviction, seven months in the federal Maxwell Prison in Alabama, and made his name synonymous with corruption.

While Watergate was believed by many to be his primary legacy, what happened after Watergate was much more significant in eternity. His arrest and complete political failure led to a change in his heart that made him open to God's grace. In 1973, while under disgrace but before his incarceration, he accepted Jesus Christ as his Lord and Savior. It was a decision that would shape the rest of his life.

After getting out of prison, Colson founded Prison Fellowship, when prison ministry was an afterthought in the United States. Colson's organization would establish and transform prison ministries all over the country, touching millions of lives. According to a brief biography of this amazing man on the Colson Center for Christian Worldview website, Colson visited over 600 prisons in the U.S. and 40 other countries, building a movement that at one time extended to more than 50,000 prison ministry volunteers.

As if this wasn't enough, he was also active in lobbying for important legislation to improve prison conditions and wrote numerous books, essays, and articles. In many ways, he became our nation's conscience for ethics and reform in the judicial system.

For his service, Colson received the Templeton Prize for Progress in Religion in 1993, the Presidential Citizens Medal in 2008, the Humanitarian Award from Domino's Pizza Corporation in 1991, the Others Award from the Salvation Army in 1990, Acton Institute's Faith & Freedom Award in 1993, and numerous honorary doctorates from various colleges and universities.

When he received the Temple Prize in Religion award, he donated its one-million-dollar prize to Prison Fellowship. While one of the most sought-after speakers in the country, he never set a fee for speaking and donated all his speaking fees and book royalties to Prison Fellowship, choosing to live off his salary instead.[1]

Compare Colson's experience with one of my failures in seminary. My future wife was studying to become a social worker, so I decided to take a course in church social ministries. That summer, I overextended myself and appealed to drop the class. When my appeal was denied, I dropped the class anyway, understanding I would fail. The only consequence of my failure was a slightly lower grade point average, resulting in a question on a job interview a few years later. My prospective employer had been looking at my transcripts and he asked me about the one lonely "F."

Which failure was worse, Colson's or mine? Which failure resulted in the more powerful change for the better? While we all want our failures to be as harmless as my failed class, we don't always get to pick the results of our actions. I believe Chuck Colson's world crumbled because God had greater, more amazing plans for him than a lifetime fighting political battles. Despite the horrendous failure of Watergate, his life was to become a living example of God's wisdom and intervention. "And we know that God causes all things to work together for good to those who love God, to those who are called according to his purpose" (Romans 8:28).

The book of Genesis tells us about a man whose life experience eerily mirrors Colson's in many ways. Joseph was also imprisoned, and yet God used him to change many, many lives. This similarity is amazing because their lives could not have been more different, and Joseph's failure was much less severe than Colson's. Joseph's failure occurred when he told his brothers about dreams in which they symbolically bowed down to him. His brothers were already upset with Joseph because of their father's favoritism, and Joseph should probably have been a little humbler and more sensitive to other people's feelings.

The favoritism of his father and the telling of the dreams had serious consequences for Joseph. His brothers, still furious at the "dreamer," sold him to some Midianite traders who took him to Egypt where he was sold to Pharaoh's captain of the guard. While Joseph's hard work was recognized and rewarded by his master, Joseph ended up in even more trouble when he was falsely accused of attempted rape by his master's wife. Because of her accusations, Joseph was imprisoned. Altogether, Joseph spent thirteen years as a household slave or in prison before he was elevated to a position of honor over Pharaoh's food supply.

As bad as Joseph's situation became, his story had a happy ending. While imprisoned, Joseph successfully interpreted dreams. As a result, Joseph was given a powerful position of authority in Pharaoh's court, which allowed him to save millions of people from starvation, including his own family.

Both Chuck Colson and Joseph failed. Mr. Colson was directly responsible for his failure, and he failed in an extraordinary, very public way. Joseph was also responsible for his failure, but he failed in a very private, seemingly insignificant way. Both failures had immense consequences. The immediate consequences were horrible for both men—incarceration and public humiliation. The long-term consequences were amazing and transformed their worlds.

If all our failures were like my failed class, insignificant without significant consequences, or if God did not use our failures to His glory through the Ministry of Failure, what would life be like? I am not sure, but I shudder at the thought. We don't like painful consequences, but they are unavoidable and for our ultimate good.

Some people live like there were no consequences to failure. Samson was one such man. Before he was even conceived, an angel appeared to Samson's parents announcing his birth. The angel told the parents to be careful how they raised the child, because the child would be a Nazirite from birth. A Nazirite was a person set aside to God for a predetermined amount of time. There were three commitments every Nazirite was expected to fulfill.

They were not to drink or eat anything made from grapes or grape bi-products.

They were not to cut their hair for the duration of their commitment.

They were not to have contact with any dead bodies or graves.

A person would remain a Nazirite, "holy to the Lord," until their vow was fulfilled by offering a special sacrifice in the temple.

The angel made it clear Samson was to be a permanent Nazarite—a Nazarite for life.

Samson's life was noted for several things in addition to his Nazirite vow. He was extremely strong. He was extremely stubborn. He lived for the moment, usually without thought of consequences. He treated his parents like servants and the enemies of God like friends, until they betrayed him, and then he got revenge unmercifully. Even the Nazarene vows meant nothing to him.

Based on his lifestyle, the only part of the vow he likely kept was his long hair. Once it was cut, he lost his power, was captured by his "friends," had his eyes gouged out, was imprisoned, and then kept as a slave and an object of ridicule. His final act when his hair began to regrow was to use his returning strength to bring down a building where he was on display, killing everyone in it—including himself. Living like there are no consequences often brings the worst consequences upon us.

Samson is not alone. Consider the life of Karla Faye Tucker. She was a drug addict whose drug use made her feel indestructible. On June 13, 1983 Karla Faye, Danny Garrett, and James Leibrant brutally murdered two people, Jerry Lynn Dean and Deborah Thornton. Karla committed the actual murders with a pickax. Tucker later told investigators that she got sexual satisfaction with every strike of the pickax. The next day the pickax was found still lodged in the chest of Deborah Thornton.[3]

Karla Faye was arrested for first-degree murder, convicted, and on April 25, 1984 was sentenced to death. In an interview with CNN, Karla said that about three months after she was arrested, a puppet ministry came to her jail. Karla went because she was feeling lonely. Once she came in to the service, instead of socializing, she stole a Bible and went back to her cell.

> I didn't know that they gave out Bibles free in here to those who needed them. So, I took this Bible into my cell, and I hid way back in the corner so nobody could see me, because I was like really proud. I didn't want anybody to think I was being weak and reading this Bible. I realize now, you have to be stronger to walk with the Lord in here than you do to not walk with Him. It's a whole lot harder, let me tell you. But anyway, that night I started reading the Bible. I didn't know what I was reading and before I knew it, I was just—I was in the middle of my floor on my knees and I was asking God to forgive me.[4]

Every indication is that this conversion was genuine. The change in her was so drastic and so consistent that, despite the heinous nature of her crime, she became the poster child for the anti-capital punishment movement. Thousands of people eventually fought for her stay of execution. Even Pat Robertson of the 700 Club came to her defense, appealing for mercy. Nonetheless, Karla Faye Tucker was executed February 3, 1998 by lethal injection in Texas.

Even if she had won a stay of execution, it would not have undone the consequences of her crime. Jerry Lynn Dean and Deborah Thornton were both still dead, torn needlessly out of their grieving families' lives. Tucker's partner, Daniel Ryan Garrett, had not gone to the house that night intending to kill anyone and yet, because of Karla's bloodlust, ended up dying of liver failure in prison. Becoming a Christian does not mean we are exempt from the overwhelming consequences of failure, whether our failure occurs before or after our salvation.

How many people get divorced or go bankrupt and then grieve over the high financial and relational consequences? Failure has consequences.

My wife and I once had a landlord whose business partner embezzled a significant amount of money and disappeared. At the same time, my landlord's wife came down with a life-threatening disease. Because of the embezzlement, my landlord paid his wife's hospital bill with money that was intended for the Internal Revenue Service. When he failed to pay his taxes, the IRS did not care about his noble cause—saving the life of his wife—or the injustice of the embezzlement. They pursued him with a vengeance until he paid every cent.

It doesn't matter who we are, what we believe, Christian or non-Christian, rich or poor, young or old, how major our failure is, or whether we are at fault or not, consequences of failure are inevitable and usually beyond our control.

Too often, we are like Achan, a man who disobeyed God and then tried to cover up his failure by burying the evidence (Joshua 7). His life did not end well. Ananias and Sapphira are two more people who experienced devastating consequences as a result of their deception (Acts 5). These biblical stories remind us that nobody wants the negative consequences of failure, and sometimes we are willing to suffer tremendous internal guilt and turmoil as we bury the evidence.

My brother's roommate, whom I will call Steve, was arrested and spent nine years in prison for transporting a plane full of cocaine. He agreed to fly the plane from Florida to Texas for one million dollars. When he got in the plane, he immediately knew there wasn't enough fuel, but the smugglers put a gun to his head and refused to delay take-off. The plane ran out of fuel during bad weather in Mississippi and crashed into a swamp. The only thing that saved Steve's life was the fact that his plane was being followed by the FBI.

My brother, Alan, was shocked when the FBI showed up at his apartment and found a huge amount of money under his roommate's bed. They also asked my brother about an extremely expensive sports car that had recently been purchased in Alan's name. Needless to say, my brother was happy to disavow any relationship to the car.

When we fail, we sometimes try to hide the evidence of our failure under our bed or we try to put the evidence in another person's name. We act as though nothing happened or try to blame people, circumstances, or even God Himself, rather than face up to the reality of our failure. When we do, we temporarily replace the natural consequences of our actions and imprison ourselves through stress, broken relationships, ulcers, secret guilt, headaches, and self-deception. In addition, if and when our failure is finally revealed, the consequences can be that much greater.

An ancient saying that we don't hear much anymore is "don't kick against the goads." A goad is a long, slender pole, sharpened at one end and used by a farmer to direct his oxen as they plow. If an ox responds to the painful prodding by kicking out, he often suffers much greater harm. Consequences are often God's goad in our life. When we are goaded, we don't benefit from ignoring or fighting against the source of our pain. Instead, we need to face our failures and consider carefully how to best react to any resulting consequences.

We also need to be careful not to focus all our attention on the negative consequences of our failures. There is much to be learned from failure, and God's grace is a powerful and usually unexpected consequence. In God's economy, even the nation-shaking consequences of Watergate have been overshadowed by the spiritual impact of Prison Fellowship on the lives of hundreds of thousands of prisoners over the last forty-one years. When we open our eyes to see what God is doing, we learn that God uses the consequences of our failure, great or small, to His glory.

61

This hope of God's grace is what gave King David the courage, even after he committed adultery and murderous betrayal, to pray the following:

> Behold, You desire truth in the innermost being,
> And in the hidden part You will make me know wisdom.
> Purify me with hyssop, and I shall be clean;
> Wash me, and I shall be whiter than snow.
> Make me to hear joy and gladness,
> Let the bones which You have broken rejoice.
> Hide Your face from my sins
> And blot out all my iniquities.
> Create in me a clean heart, O God,
> And renew a steadfast spirit within me.
> (Psalm 51:6-10)

God's grace is greater than any failure.

Dave's Story

I was raised in a Christian home, going to church on a regular basis. My parents were good Christian people, but my father did have a tendency to follow preachers, including some who were very legalistic in their approach. I remember going home many nights afraid to go to sleep because of hell fire and damnation. This environment led to my brothers and me rebelling against the gospel. Even though my parents sent me to Christian schools, I caused so much trouble by tenth grade that I was kicked out.

Finishing up tenth grade in public schools, I managed to stay out of trouble. But by eleventh grade I gave in to the parties, the alcohol, and the girls. I loved beer. I remember the first time I drank a beer. I was seventeen and coming up a hill that I know well since I drive it regularly. One beer led to another. When I was on my second or third beer, I remember thinking I'm going to like this, and it is going to cause a lot of problems for me.

From then on, high school was mainly beer, partying, and out-of-control behavior.

I met my first wife while still in high school, and we married young. I was twenty and she was two years behind me. We were only married two and a half or three years. The marriage's failure was both our faults, but I was more the culprit. My drinking just continued to grow. I loved to drink.

The divorce was extremely difficult on me because I was still dealing with the guilt and remorse from my legalistic upbringing. Divorce seemed like the end of the world. It was like a death in the family. I didn't love well, but I loved my wife. I think she would have said the same at the time. I just didn't know how to love her correctly. When you lose someone you have been in love with for four or five years it is devastating. It caused me to increase my drinking, and I graduated to hard liquor.

During that time of separation and divorce, my bad personal relationships increased. You are not going to meet wholesome people in drunken environments. You are not going to do that. That doesn't mean I was a good person, because I surely wasn't, but my problems just continually perpetuated once I started drinking liquor. Not only did I lose relationships, I lost good jobs. People thought I was a good worker. For example, I worked for twelve years at a local factory. I had good reports until my tenth year, and then feedback wasn't too good. At first, I would show up for work hungover, and then I began showing up for work drunk. I eventually lost that job and began living in a hotel. Despite my lack of income, my drinking still increased because I was drawing unemployment. I also had money from some retirement funds that I drank away. In the meantime, if I needed a few dollars, I would work some part-time jobs until they fired me. I couldn't count how many jobs I lost over that time.

As my alcoholism progressed, I was arrested and imprisoned for DUI, driving with a suspended license, and resisting arrest. The resisting arrest charge took place when a friend of my ex-wife's pulled me over. He was apparently trying to take her out at the time and made a comment that made me mad, and I pushed him. While that is enough for a felony charge of assault, they knocked it down to resisting arrest, because the policeman I pushed was pretty aggressive. I am not blaming the police officer. It was a bad situation, and I didn't make it any better. You don't have much sense when you're drinking and you're twenty-eight years old and hell bent on being hell bent. So, from the age of twenty-three to thirty-three years old, I was in prison three different times.

I was also in four different rehabs. One I shouldn't even count because I left after less than twenty-four hours. The rehabs were generally for about thirty days, and they were mostly work mandated. If I didn't do them I would lose my job. One of the jobs I took during this period was up in the county home as a nursing assistant. I stayed sober for about three months, and they loved me until I started drinking. I would drink vodka to try and cover up the smell. I was told you could not smell it, but you can. They went from loving me to loathing me in a year's time.

Wherever I worked during this time, I would end up with a series of bad emotional relationships and eventually a bad job situation. It always started off well. I would sober up for a few months, and then I would be back at it. Then my sister died when she was just twenty-five. She was a good Christian girl who had suffered from a brain tumor for four years. I used her death to blame God.

Afterward, when I was sober, I would search the Bible to prove it was wrong. I didn't search much because my drinking increased and, to make matters worse, I began using cocaine, marijuana, and pills. I stayed away from needles because I was a little squeamish about them. Twice, I ended up in a psych ward in York Hospital. I bet I had the DTs 200 times in my life. That is how many times I needed alcohol and couldn't get it, couldn't afford it, or was trying to quit. The amazing thing is just one DT episode can kill you. Coming off alcohol and heroin are the same. It is a bad withdrawal that can kill you.

The last two years of my drinking binge were from the age of thirty-one to thirty-three. I ended up living under a bridge in York, Pennsylvania, for about nine months. I was homeless because I chose to be homeless. I couldn't afford regular alcohol, so I would steal rubbing alcohol from the local pharmacies, and I learned how to drink diluted anti-freeze. This hard-core drinking resulted in me ending up in the hospital with damage to my central nervous system.

The last time I ended up in the psych ward of the hospital, my father came. He was as disappointed as he could and should be. He said he was going to leave me at the psych ward unless I could tell him I was at least going to make an attempt at changing. A pastor friend of mine from a local church also came. He prayed with me and we talked a little. By this time, I didn't have a mother, brothers, or sisters. Everybody had forsaken me, and I don't blame them one bit. I prayed to God, "Lord I don't want to live like this anymore."

For the next two weeks I continued my search in Scripture, looking for error, but only seeing truth. There were two miracles during this time. My eyes were opened and Scripture became clear to me. And I did not have the DTs upon my release like I had so many times before. I wasn't home free, however. While Scriptures were becoming clear, they were also very discouraging because I began bearing the weight of what I had done with my life. I was beginning to own as much responsibility as I could at that time in my life. I realized I couldn't fault my past and blame it on what people had done to me. All the weight for my mistakes, sins, failures, and disappointments came upon me.

I also had a determination to get right with God that I had never had before. Six months afterwards, however, I had a failure

65

where I went out on a two or three-day binge. That same pastor who had visited me in the psych ward came to me and said, "Dave, Satan wants you to think you are not saved. He wants you to think you are a failure." He said, "Get back up. Pick yourself up, dust yourself off, and start all over again." That was it. That was twenty-four years ago, and the last time drugs and alcohol had total control over my life.

Don't misunderstand, it took a while. I had so much physical damage, so much mental damage. I couldn't hold a thought for too long. When I came home from the psych ward, I was in diapers, because I couldn't control my bowels or my bladder. They diagnosed me with liver damage. I was a mess. Once my thought life started to clear up, however, I started centering my thoughts around God's Word, focusing more on God's truth than my past or my present desires. Matthew 6:24-34 became extremely important to me. Through this Scripture I realized I shouldn't focus on sobriety. I should focus on my relationship with Christ first and then sobriety would follow. I still strongly desired alcohol, but God was teaching me to change my patterns.

An important part of changing my patterns was to put roadblocks in my own path. When I was thirty-seven, my family wanted me to move in with them in order to keep myself clean. For two or three months I did move home, but God convicted me I needed to do this on my own without being sheltered by everyone. So, I moved away from my family. While my family was terrified I was moving away in order to self-destruct, I was smart enough to not move close to a tap room. I put roadblocks in my way to protect myself.

I wasn't driving at the time, so I would have had to walk some five miles to get a drink. I didn't trust myself. I also made a commitment to share everything with my sobriety sponsor. He was a Christian accountability partner who I shared everything with, including my temptations and my schemes to get my next drink. We met once a week at first. Later, as I became more successful, we met once a month. While I thought I was over the hump after the first year of sobriety, I knew I had to have someone to be accountable to. I also knew I had to continue to put roadblocks in my path and to seek God and His face every day. God had to come first.

After two or three months of reading the Bible, I was no longer in diapers. I could hold a thought in my head. When I first started studying Scripture, I read it with a legalistic mindset because that was how I was raised. As I read, however, God started dismantling my approach. I saw things I had never seen before, and I had an epiphany. I realized faith isn't avoiding sin. It is asserting your relationship with Christ. Faith is not about what you don't do. Faith is about doing. It is about your relationship with Christ and in doing that, other things fall by the wayside.

I replaced my passion for drinking with my passion for the Word of God. While it was a lifeline for me, I believe I actually read too much. I probably read 50-100 chapters a day. I also read two or three men's books a week. God convicted me I wasn't retaining it. He showed me I needed to use the Scripture and the truths I was reading to learn to think for myself.

Once I put God first and I focused on following Him, sobriety eventually followed along. There is a program, Celebrate Recovery, which follows that same principle. While I am okay with the Alcoholics Anonymous program, I try to encourage others towards the Celebrate Recovery program. Even with a focus on God, it took a couple years for a real sense of sobriety to take hold of me.

While I was glad to be sober, there were still consequences of my drinking I had to live with. Some of my relationships with my family weren't restored for two or three years. While I didn't blame them, it was difficult having brothers not speak to me. My mother didn't speak to me for a year. I think my isolation was harder after I was converted because I knew my change was real. But my relatives, especially those who were in the church, had seen me try to sober up before on my own, and they were waiting for me to fail. I would hear comments like, "Well, we will see how long this will last." Even when the Lord is with you, you don't always have a sense of His presence, and it is a very lonely time when you don't have family at your back.

I can't blame them for not understanding. I still don't understand my addiction. I understand it was the love of my life, and I loved it more than life itself. I understand I was willing to do anything to drink. At the same time, I don't understand. How can I expect other people to?

Within six to eight months I was taking Bible courses. Within two years I was taking seminary courses. I wouldn't go back to drinking because I love my relationship with the Lord and also because I love thinking clearly. I went fifteen years when I couldn't think clearly. All I thought about was when was I going to get drunk next or when was I going to have a good time. What an awful way to live.

Eventually, I began ministering to people who had problems like my own. I began going to Bible studies and got involved in prison ministry. I met Tina in a Bible study. Our church had a big brother program and I became a big brother to her son. She invited me over for dinner one night, and we eventually started dating. She helped me minister in a prison for a while, and then we worked together in a rehab called Lydia's Center for Women. I became their chaplain, and she was a counselor.

Even though I was determined to never get married again because I wasn't very successful in relationships, Tina and I eventually married. Ministering with Tina and my father for the last fifteen years of his life has been a blessed trip. At the same time, it has been a rough ride at times. Christianity can be as difficult as the world can be, a lot of challenges. Faith is not

68

knowing what tomorrow holds. It is knowing who holds tomorrow and that you can trust Him.

In the Bible there is a story of a prodigal son who wasted his inheritance only to eventually return home to his father and brother. It is the story of how his life was turned around. At the end of the story there are two brothers. People don't realize that if this is where the story ends, the prodigal son is eternally much better off than his brother who stayed at home. The outside world will look at that and say, "No! No! No!" but that kind of example is repeated in other Scriptures such as the story of David and Saul. Saul's life appeared better to others, but God saw David was repentant while Saul wasn't. For that reason, I thank God I was an alcoholic. Not because it was pleasant to anybody, but because it brought me to God and taught me a great deal.

People have different struggles. Alcoholism happened to be mine. Honestly, it wasn't even a struggle. I submitted to it. I drank myself into alcoholism one choice at a time. I wasn't born craving alcohol. There are tendencies and some people can resist it, but it is a matter of choices. Now, I did get to a point where I was so physically dependent I needed it to live. If I didn't have alcohol I would go into convulsions. Coming to that point didn't just happen, though. It was a result of a long string of choices. I was recently talking to a guy in prison who was sad because he said he wasted ten years of his life, and I had the opportunity to tell him I had done the same thing, but I had begun thinking of these years, not as lost years, but as learning time.

Some of the things I learned are that it is important not to live in the past. The past is done. Paul talked about putting those things behind you—God's way is better. Even if I want to do things my way, I often choose to do things God's way, not because I am such a good Christian but because I don't feel like going through that again.

I learned God loves you just where you are, but He also loves you too much to leave you where you are. I learned God has to come even before your own family, and I learned to be more sympathetic of other people's failures, sins, and situations. Their struggles might be gluttony or cheating other people out of money or any other sin. I am not too quick to criticize, especially addicts and drunks who truly want to change and can't. It's difficult, but that is the nature of sin. I also learned you can't hide from the world, and that God can use me despite my past.

Recently, I was blessed to experience God using me as a result of a box of Bibles donated to the York Prison. We had three or four boxes from random churches. I picked up one Bible and noticed it was a King James Bible and had an inscription. When I read the inscription, I thought, You have got to be kidding me! Forty-eight years ago, my parents gave us kids Bibles inscribed with our names. My brother is a tough man who resists God at every corner. Now, almost fifty years later, I am reading the inscription and Bible dedication from my parents to my brother. If that ain't a God-thing, I don't know what is. I know we are in the same area, but that Bible is fifty years old, and my brother hadn't picked up a Bible ... How it got in there ... I put it away and gave it to him a few days later. He said, "Well, that is not a big deal." Considering the journeys taken to get this Bible back to him— my journey and the Bible's journey—I think he realized that it was a big deal. I left it on his car seat.

Author's Note: David Hildebrand currently serves as one of two chaplains for the 2,522 men and women in the York County Prison in York, Pennsylvania. In the past sixteen years, he has worshiped with, met one-on-one with, and held Bible studies with more than 14,000 inmates. To this day, he meets men with whom he was imprisoned. Unfortunately, these men are too often trapped in a cycle of repeat offenses. He smiles when they exclaim in shock, "You're not the chaplain!"

Dave is also largely responsible for the title of this book. During our interview, Dave talked about how both the Bible's shepherd David and the prodigal son were changed by their repentant hearts and ultimately better off spiritually than either the wealthy King Saul or the comfortable son who stayed at home. When chaplain Dave said, "I thank God I was an alcoholic for that reason," I was stunned. As I wondered at the ramifications of this amazing comment, I realized how many times in my interviews I had heard other people express similar appreciation for failures that led them to God's ministry of transforming grace. I don't believe Dave was minimizing the pain of alcoholism, either to himself or others. Rather, he was testifying to an experience of God's grace so powerful that it was worth any failure or pain.

Meditation Moment

- Charles Stanley once said, "One of Satan's most deceptive and powerful ways of defeating us is to get us to believe a lie. And the biggest lie is that there are no consequences to our own doing. Satan will give you whatever you ask for if it will lead you where he ultimately wants you."5 Has there ever been a time in your life when you experienced the powerful deception of "the biggest lie?"

- Achan was motivated to cover up his moral failure by greed. Ananias and Sapphira were motivated by spiritual pride and greed. King David probably imagined himself protected by the power of the monarchy. At times in your life when you have covered up your personal failures, what has been your greatest motivation? Is there a "cover up" in your life you need to confess to God or to someone else?

- Galatians 6:7-8 gives us the principle of sowing and reaping. "Do not be deceived, God is not mocked; for

71

whatever a man sows, this he will also reap. For the one who sows to his own flesh will from the flesh reap corruption, but the one who sows to the Spirit will from the Spirit reap eternal life." Consequences of our actions can be positive or negative. They will always exist. What can you do today to sow to the Spirit?

- What is God doing in your life right now?

Chapter Five

Failure and Pride

*When I focus with pleasure on my dignity, my accomplishments,
my importance and my abilities, I am in a dangerous place.*

He was a successful banker. As he stood before his boss and his
associates, he was stripped of every vestige of pride that he
possessed. They took his corsage and ripped it in half. Earlier in
the day his failure had caused a run on the bank. They broke his
umbrella. His son had tuppence (two pennies) that he wanted to
feed the pigeons with instead of investing. They broke his bowler
hat. When he tried to take the tuppence from his son, his son
hollered out, resulting in panic among the patrons of the bank.
That night, the man was called on the carpet. When his boss, Mr.
Dawes, asked Mr. Banks if he had anything to say before his
dismissal, Mr. Banks reached into his pocket and pulled out the
coins that had started this disaster. Looking at the small coins, he
seemed to lose his mind and said the only thing left to say,
"supercalifragilisticexpialidocious."

In the final scene of the movie, Mr. Banks is joyfully flying a
kite with the family that he, in his drive for success, had almost
destroyed. Mary Poppins flies off, her job done. The father is
humbled, his priorities are straightened out, he is offered a
partnership in the bank, and his family is healed. What makes a
delightful family musical, sometimes makes a painful reality.

Three men stood up in a business meeting and called for my
dismissal as pastor. I knew they were going to and why they
were doing it. Since I knew this was coming, one of our
denominational leaders, Stan Smith, led the meeting, which did
not make it any easier. To make matters worse, the congregation

sat in stunned silence. When my opportunity to take the floor came, I stood and read a carefully prepared defense of my ministry for the past year. Later, my wife also stood to defend me. Some of my best friends and strongest church leaders said nothing. By the time the business meeting was over, I was retained as pastor, and the church was committed to conflict training and mediation with the Peacemaker's ministry.

The next week I met with Stan, the moderator of the meeting, to supposedly discuss the meeting and the path forward. The truth was, I wanted another chance to make sure he understood what led up to the meeting and how I was completely in the right. Our conversation did not go exactly as planned. What he said stunned me and left me that way for days as I processed his evaluation.

When I started to defend myself, he cut me off and said, "Carl, you missed a great opportunity Sunday to provide your church with leadership. All you had to do was encourage them and say, 'We can get through this together.' Instead, you defended yourself, and I noticed no one else except your wife said a thing." I really don't remember the rest of our conversation. There were all kinds of things I wanted to say to him, but I knew in my heart he was right. Something was terribly wrong with my ministry.

For days I thought about Jesus standing before His accusers saying nothing. I thought about the pride that motivated my defense. I thought about why the church was stunned and silent in the face of my accusers. Mentally processing my failure was even more difficult than the business meeting. I had no self-righteousness to hide behind. I could not say it was my accusers' fault, because nothing I was struggling with had anything to do with them.

Our church had a leadership team entrusted with supervising the overall church mission. As I thought back to the past year, I realized there had been increasingly serious problems and conflicts within the congregation which I addressed on my own in the name of confidentiality. Unfortunately, these situations just kept compounding and finally reached the point where they threatened the witness of the church. Just as I was preparing to involve the leadership team, parties involved in these situations called for my dismissal.

The pride which led me to handle these problems on my own, and my subsequent culpability in laying the ground work for a major church conflict, overwhelmed me. I had failed in my primary pastoral calling. I had been more of a Lone Ranger than a shepherd protecting his sheep. Shepherds frequently bring their herds together, especially in the evening when the danger is greatest, so they can work together to provide security. Whether you call them elders, deacons, or a leadership team, every pastor needs the support of co-shepherds who can help protect the flock.

We use the word pride and the word proud in a number of different ways. We use them to refer to a sense of satisfaction and well-being we get from seeing the accomplishment of others. I am, for example, proud of my sons for what they have done—for being close to God, for running an ultra-marathon, for getting a black belt, for getting good grades, and for playing soccer, just to name a few of their accomplishments. I am proud of a friend for being one of the top swimmers in the nation. I am proud of my wife for being an amazing animal-assisted play therapist. We use the word pride to refer to a sense of satisfaction and well-being we get from being part of a community. Hence, the Beach Boys' "Be True to Your School," where students' pride in their school inspires them to stand up to a loud braggart.

These types of pride may or may not be sinful, but when that sense of satisfaction and well-being we call pride finds its source internally, we are squarely in the Culture of Success. When I focus with pleasure on my dignity, my accomplishments, my importance, and my abilities, I am in a dangerous place. As it says in Proverbs 16:18, "Pride goes before destruction, and a haughty spirit before stumbling."

Failure and pride are antithetical, yet pride leads to failure.

The children of Israel had seen amazing miracles, including the plagues of Egypt and the parting of the Red Sea. God Himself had spoken to them from the top of a mountain. Their leader Moses met with God and even had to cover his face at times because it shone with the glory of God. Yes, they had been slaves, but look how far they had come. Yes, they were still in the wilderness, but God Himself was guiding them and feeding them. Unfortunately, their pride threatened their very existence as the children of God. I Corinthians 10:1-4 is the story of this pride. It begins by talking about the wilderness miracles.

For I do not want you to be unaware, brethren, that our fathers were all under the cloud and all passed through the sea; and all were baptized into Moses in the cloud and in the sea; and all ate the same spiritual food; and all drank the same spiritual drink, for they were drinking from a spiritual rock which followed them; and the rock was Christ.

What would it have been like to have seen the wonders this passage is referring to? Except for the era of Jesus and His disciples, there has never been a generation which experienced such an abundance of miracles.

Speaking of this passage, Matthew Henry once wrote, "Judaism was Christianity under a veil, wrapped up in types and dark hints."6 In other words, their miraculous experiences reflect what God wants to do in the life of every follower of Jesus Christ. God is still the God of the miraculous, and sometimes all He wants us to do is wait on Him to part the sea and follow Him as He leads the way.

Just as miracles were most prevalent in the early days of Israel and in the early days of the Church, miracles are often most prevalent in the early days of an individual's decision to follow

Jesus. No matter how many children a parent may have, it is natural to pay extra attention to newborn babies. I believe sometimes our heavenly Father performs miracles in order to encourage the faith of His newly born children.

One of my favorite examples is how God provided my financial needs when I began seminary. Still a young Christian, I believed there was enough money to last until getting a paycheck from substitute teaching. Unfortunately, there were unexpected costs involved with enrolling into school and moving into a new apartment. The money quickly ran out. The school district I was working for also structured their pay schedule for substitute teachers so my first check would not come for almost four months after my arrival.

I was going to school full-time, working part-time at a job which would not pay for months, and out of money. For months I waited and God provided. While my diet consisted primarily of peanut butter and jelly sandwiches and canned mackerel (it was cheap), I experienced an amazing sense of peace and did not tell anyone about my financial problems. I cannot tell you how many people invited me over to eat or gave me part-time jobs.

One day I was out of money and wasn't sure my car had enough gas to drive to school when a friend called and offered me a job digging ditches. I loved working for him, because he paid in cash. After he paid me, I went straight to the gas station where my car ran out of gas as it coasted up to the gas pump (this actually happened twice).

After three months, I wrote my father asking him for help, and he sent me twenty bucks. It was enough to wash my clothes and keep me in canned mackerel until my paycheck arrived. God's timely provision is just one of the many miracles I have had the joy of experiencing. It turned a challenging time in my life into one of my dearest memories.

While Israel experienced an abundance of miracles in their early days of following God, they reacted poorly to God's blessings at times. Their prideful reaction serves to warn us today of what happens when we, as believers, adopt a similar attitude.

Nevertheless, with most of them God was not well-pleased; for they were laid low in the wilderness. Now these things happened as examples for us, so that we would not crave evil things as they also craved. (1 Corinthians 10:5-6)

What were the evil things which resulted in the death of virtually an entire generation in the wilderness? Let's look at a few. Idolatry

"Do not be idolaters, as some of them were; as it is written, 'The people sat down to eat and drink, and stood up to play'" (vs. 7).

Success leads us to believe we have a right to "eat, drink and be merry." After all, haven't we earned our blessings? In some ways the children of Israel were like modern America as they traveled around the wilderness. Between setting up camp and tearing it down, they had a lot of free time and a lot of money given to them as they left Egypt.

When you have wealth and the time to enjoy it, it is easy to neglect your relationship with God, especially when you are already proud of how good you are and how much you have accomplished. We neglect worship because we can worship God wherever we are and in whatever we are doing. We neglect prayer because we are too busy playing. We neglect His Word because our days are filled going from one activity to the next. Our pride sets us up for spiritual failure.

Immorality

"Nor let us act immorally, as some of them did, and twenty-three thousand fell in one day" (vs. 8).

This verse refers to an incident in Numbers 25. Some Israelites accepted an invitation to join the Moabites in a sacrificial feast. Unfortunately, the feast was to the Moabite God Baal who was the ancient god of fertility. Public acts of sex with temple prostitutes were supposed to encourage Baal to provide rain and fertility for a bountiful harvest. A barbecue. Plenty of wine. Public sex. An ancient version of Woodstock.

One thing about pride, it helps us rationalize any sin. Just consider the Motion Picture Association of America film rating system that has become such an important part of our life. There is a subtle message in this system. Maturity equals the ability to watch inappropriate content. Limiting your visual intake to PG or PG-13 means you are not mature enough to handle the adult stuff. Pride says, "I am an adult, and I can watch whatever I want. I can handle it."

"For ... the boastful pride of life, is not from the Father, but is from the world" (I John 2:16).

Ungratefulness

"Nor let us try the Lord, as some of them did, and were destroyed by the serpents" (vs 9).

This verse is a reference to an incident which occurred after the nation had been wondering around the wilderness for what seemed like a long time. "The people spoke against God and Moses, 'Why have you brought us up out of Egypt to die in the wilderness? For there is no food and no water, and we loathe this miserable food'" (Numbers 21:5).

There was food. There was water as they needed it, and they were better off than under Egyptian slavery. Their pride had given them blessing amnesia which led them to the mistaken belief they deserved better than God's provision. It took a plague of serpents to wake them up to their need.

Complaining

"Nor grumble, as some of them did, and were destroyed by the destroyer" (vs 10).

Complaining is an expression of human pride. I deserve better than this. Sometimes it's couched in sanctimonious concern for others. We deserve better than this.

When we struggle with any of these—idolatry, immorality, ungratefulness, and complaining—we need to remember the root is self-pride. They are the offspring of the Culture of Success, and their spiritual fruit is never good. Perhaps that is why Paul concludes this passage with an admonishment to avoid thinking we "stand" lest we "fall" (I Corinthians 10:11, 12). Areas we think are our greatest strengths can become our greatest stumbling blocks largely because they feed our sense of self pride.

"Pride and arrogance and the evil way and the perverted mouth, I hate" (Proverbs 8:13).

What God hates can't work out for our ultimate good. These heart failings eventually led the nation of Israel to rebel against God's will, which resulted in their death in the wilderness. One of the greatest blessings of failure is when it keeps us from self-pride and helps us to rely on our relationship with God more so He can lead us to His ultimate will for our life.

Job was an amazing man. In his story, we find a godly man whom God Himself praises. He is one of the wealthiest men on the earth with huge crops and a large and flourishing family. In a very short time his children are dead, his crops are stolen, his wealth is gone, his health is ruined, and his wife is telling him to curse God and die.

Three friends come and try to convince Job his sin is the cause of his misfortune. If he would only repent, God would surely restore him. When Job fails to see the error of his ways, a fourth young man makes his appeal. After everything is said and done, nothing is accomplished. Job is still in misery. His refusal to repent is a disappointment to his friends, and his wife still wants nothing to do with him.

Through all the loss, pain, rejection, and confusion, Job remained steadfast in his belief that his suffering was not a result of his own sin. In Job 13:3, Job said, "But I would speak to the Almighty, and I desire to argue with God."

Then the Lord answered Job ...
Will the faultfinder contend with the Almighty?
Let him who reproves God answer it." (Job 38:1)
Then Job answered the Lord and said,
Behold, I am insignificant; what can I reply to You?
I lay my hand on my mouth.
Once I have spoken, and I will not answer;
Even twice, and I will add nothing more."
(Job 40:1-5)

When God began speaking to Job, the change in Job was instantaneous. He saw God, and he saw his own insignificance. In his vision of God, Job finally addressed the reality of his failure. Job's pride did not lead to his failure. It was his failure. While there are many lessons from the book of Job and only God knows the reason for all of Job's sufferings, one thing is certain. God used the tragedies in his life, together with divine revelation, to drive the pride out of Job. Evidence of this new humility is in Job's cry of repentance and willingness to pray for his friends who had tormented him for so long.

I have heard of You by the hearing of the ear;
But now my eye sees You;

81

Therefore, I retract,
And I repent in dust and ashes.
(Job 42:5, 6)

The Lord restored the fortunes of Job when he prayed for his friends, and the Lord increased all that Job had twofold (see Job 42:10).

Were there negative consequences to Job's pride? Absolutely. But the long-term effect was a newfound relationship with God, one based not on the pride of success but the grace found in failure.

While my experience in the church business meeting was not nearly as severe as Job's, God is willing to use a variety of extraordinary means to help each of us address the failure of self-pride. Oftentimes these means are circumstances beyond our control.

Consider, for example, a surrogate father I had while attending college. He was a wonderful, cheerful man of incredible energy who worked himself up to director of sales in one of the nation's largest bus terminals. As such, he became friends with the president of the corporation. When this president tried unsuccessfully to become the chairman of the board, the surviving chairman of the board purged everyone the president was associated with. While my surrogate father wasn't fired, he was demoted to bag boy in the same station he worked in.

I remember the pain and struggle of his "Job experience" as he sent out his resume and prayed about what God wanted him to do. I cannot imagine what God must have done in his heart to get him to accept His revealed will. One day he declared to us that God had made it clear he was to stay in the company and be the best bag boy possible. He threw his heart and soul into his new job, coming home exhausted every night. He literally did the work of two or three people. Because of his humble spirit and hard work, it wasn't long before he was promoted to assistant manager. His story was also noticed by another busing company—which hired him—and for which he enjoyed working the rest of his career.

There is nothing easy about any failure. Pride, however, is an especially troublesome failure because by its very nature it is comfortable and content in the Culture of Success. As long as things are going well, we are satisfied to accept varying degrees of idolatry, immorality, ungratefulness, and grumbling. We are satisfied until we are confronted with major problems or even a Job experience which knocks our feet out from under us. Humility is a hard, painful lesson to learn and, unfortunately, one we are never finished learning. Helping us discover humility is an important Ministry of Failure.

Pride is also especially troubling, because it can be very deceptive. The difference between wanting your ministry, business, or team to thrive and wanting personally and proudly to be a success is one small step between serving in the Ministry of Failure and the Culture of Success.

While this motivation of pride might be normal and accepted in our society, it is a barrier to experiencing God. As C.S. Lewis once wrote, "In God, you come up against something that is in every respect immeasurably superior to yourself. Unless you know God as that and, therefore, know yourself as nothing in comparison—you do not know God at all. As long as you are proud, you cannot know God."7

Aaron's Story

For twenty years, my career with a large national bank in Florida progressed fairly smoothly. I had multiple promotions and learning opportunities. Everything changed in 2007 when I was asked to do some unscrupulous things that did not seem fair to the elderly customers we serviced. I left that "big name" bank after twenty years and was hired by a smaller, Christian-owned bank. Unfortunately, 2007 and 2008 were rough years in the financial world. The stock market was tanking, and the Florida real estate market was in free-fall. In January of 2008, I was called into my new boss's office and laid off.

Staff reduction, cost cutting, last-hired-first-fired, laid off … call it what you want. In my mind I was a failure. I was forty-six years old with a mortgage, a wife, and six children to support (the oldest was about to start college), and I felt like I had just failed them all. In thirty years I'd never been without a job, and certainly never been fired.

Fortunately for me, my wife was very supportive. I think her exact words were, "None of this took the Lord by surprise. I can't wait to see what He has in store for us next." We continued to pray about our future, but prayer did not stop me from worrying about mortgage payments, healthcare, car insurance, food, etc.

While we were seeking the Lord, my boss called and said they had someone retire in the St. Louis office and wanted to see if I was interested in the job. While you might imagine we would jump at the opportunity, we were Floridians. All of our children had been born and raised in Florida, and we were determined to find another job in our home state. Can you imagine our frustration when—four months later with no job—my wife was waiting in food bank lines for bread and canned food just to survive. We even had neighbors leaving canned goods on our doorstep.

In God's graciousness, three times we got anonymous envelopes in the mail with $100 bills in them. But even with that and odd jobs, we were sinking. In our desperation, I was ready to do anything, so I agreed to go to Missouri—even though I had to look on the map to see where it was located.

We were sad and overwhelmed, but we committed to trust the Lord and say goodbye to our church, our home, our neighborhood, our friends, our home-school co-op, and all the sports teams the kids were participating in.

I went up ahead to start working, while my wife and children stayed behind to fix up and sell the house. The problem was, with the real estate market in crisis, the house would not sell. It took fourteen long, agonizing months. During that time, I lived in a motor home in a seedy section of St. Louis, and my wife navigated home-schooling, fixing up the house, selling off most of our possessions, all the kids' birthdays, my son's graduation, the death of our family pet, and a million other things without me. Meanwhile, I went to work every day, worried, frustrated, and utterly alone. No church, no friends, no anything.

A little voice inside my head kept telling me I was a failure. I had lost my job, my house, and even left my family behind. The fact that my family was heartbroken about being uprooted from the life (and weather) they loved, did not make things any easier. While this voice kept hammering me with guilt, the Lord kept telling me to wait upon him and my wife kept saying, "God has got this. Take it to Him in prayer."

Living in the camper did not make things any easier. In January and February, the temperature dipped to ten degrees, and all the pipes froze. In order to have running water, I had to crawl underneath the camper with a blow dryer and thaw the pipes. There were multiple occasions when I thought about packing up and going home. It was a dark, dark time, and I don't just mean my nights alone in the camper. I mean my heart, my soul, my spirit. Then God, in his faithfulness, would send a reminder that He would not "leave me or forsake me." One night, when I was convinced it was time to pack up and head home, job or no job, I got a phone call from a pastor/friend I had not spoken to in fifteen years. He said, "Is this Aaron? I have been looking for you, brother. The Lord laid you on my heart, and I wanted to call and pray with you. Tell me what is going on."

I was encouraged right then and there … and I knew I could stick it out just a little longer.

Meanwhile, back in Florida, my wife had sold most of what we owned on Craig's List in order to pay for food and insurance. Over time, she sold our furniture, toys, decorations, and even necessities. At one point, the kids said "Mom would sell the commode if someone offered to buy it." The kids still remember things they lost during that time like their big plastic cooking set they played with one day, and the next day watched some lady carry out of the house.

It took fourteen months of living apart for the house to finally sell. During that time, I couldn't even afford to travel home, so by the time we could all be together again, we didn't care if it was Missouri or the Antarctic.

When my family did join me, we all lived in the thirty-foot camper (eight people and a cat) until we could find a new home. Because we had sold everything, we only had the bare necessities on our backs. No books, no toys, no extra clothes … and we were wall-to-wall in that small space for eight weeks. When people slept on the floors at night (end to end), you could not walk across the camper. Eventually, we found a home, adjusted to our first (freezing cold) winter and snow, and started to slowly rebuild our lives in a strange new place with very little money from the crushing year we had had.

That was seven years ago now. Looking back, I see that being fired and thrown out of my comfort zone has forced me to put my selfishness and pride aside and lean on the Lord in a way I could not have formerly imagined. And God is not done yet. This lesson continues to be a daily struggle for me. While I am grateful for a job that provides for my family, I am unhappy in and question my job every day. At the same time, God has been true to his Word. My kids are in college, graduate school, the police academy, and some of them are still living at home. Most of my children will tell you the move to the Midwest has turned out to be a good thing. The Lord has given my family opportunities, blessings, and a mission field to work in. My entire family is serving in church, teaching, leading worship, and we are open to God's will for His next adventure.

Meditation Moment

- When Jesus stood before His captors before His crucifixion, men falsely accused Him. He was not alone. The Bible tells us about false accusations against many other people such as Joseph, Job, Moses, Jeremiah, Amos, Mary, Stephen, and the apostle Paul. How do you react when people accuse you of doing something you did not do? Why do you think Jesus did not respond to His accusers?

- Does pride prevent you from seeking a relationship with God on a daily basis? If so, how?

- Job experienced horrendous tragedies, loss of loved ones, loss of wealth, loss of health, rejection by his wife, and the false accusation of friends. He did not experience true humility until he saw God in His glory. Is it possible for anyone to be truly humble apart from divine intervention? What is the difference between humility, self-hatred, and self-pity? How could a relationship with God help a person keep his or her life in perspective?

- Many conflicts are the result of people proudly standing on their rights or protecting their success. Sometimes, the hardest thing to do is to stop forcing our agenda. Are you willing to put aside your own pride for the sake of seeking reconciliation with another person?

- Given the eternal perspective expressed by Psalms 103:14 which says, "we are but dust," is vanity a form of insanity? If so, what are you willing to suffer in order to be sane?

Chapter Six

Fighting the Good Fight

God is not done with us yet.

As pointed out in the introduction, there are four types of failure.

- Minor, inconsequential failures we simply do our best to avoid in the future

- Failures over which we have no control except in our reaction to resulting consequences

- Failures whose repetition can be avoided through additional education, training, and hard work

- Moral failures

Of these four types of failures, the failures that are usually the most destructive and have the most painful consequences are moral failures. To protect us against moral failures, God has given us powerful tools. When we use these tools, it is called spiritual warfare, a term which reminds me of a series of historical novels by Bernard Cornwell.

Cornwell details the 10th century wars between the Saxons and the Vikings. I love historical novels, but Cornwell's series especially fascinated me because my mother's family came to America from the land of the Vikings, and my father's family came from the land of the Brits. The history of this conflict is the history of my ancestors.

Another thing that caught my attention was the manner of their warfare. Both cultures developed and used a shield wall as their primary battle strategy. The shield wall was apparently a variation of the Roman testudo formation. Shields were linked together in front, above and to the sides of the military formation. As the enemy approached, weapons were thrust through, above, and under the shields, while men on the front line within the formation were protected by the men behind them.

In this form of warfare, there were four things each warrior trusted to protect him in the battle: his fellow warriors, his shield, his armor, and his weapon. We can liken these to the tools God has given us in our spiritual battle against moral failure.

A warrior's neighbor – accountability

A warrior's shield and armor – our faith relationship with God

A warrior's weapon – God's Word

Before we examine each of these elements, it is important to consider their significance. The Bible was written by people who struggled with the same struggles we encounter, and it is brutally honest about their failures. One of these failures occurred late in David's life. The Bible gives us an interesting picture of what led up to this epic failure.

The book of II Samuel tells us that when it was time for Israel's army to go to war, David chose to stay in Jerusalem and send the army into battle without him. While we might think that was the king's prerogative, King David wasn't just any king. He was the king of God's people. As God's people, Israel should never have been asked to fight any battle unless it was God's battle. In other words, all of their battles should have been spiritual warfare.

When King David stayed behind, he symbolically abdicated his role in spiritual warfare, relying on other people to fight for him.

The rest of the story is not pretty. Because he stayed behind, David committed adultery, betrayed one of his most loyal men, and covered up his sin by having the man killed in battle. We lay the groundwork for serious consequences when we don't care enough to fight for what is right. Relying on other people, whether they are a spouse, a friend, or a pastor, to fight your spiritual battles is a recipe for disaster.

If we are going to fight our own spiritual battles, we have to be committed to paying the cost of spiritual involvement. King David was never the same again after this experience. Only God knows how much richer his life could have been had he gone out and fought the fight which was before him.

A Warrior's Neighbor – Accountability

The first form of protection—accountability—plays a crucial role in helping break the cycle of failure. While there is no place in the Bible where God says, "thou shalt have an accountability partner," the Bible establishes principles which naturally lead to serving one another through accountability. First, the Bible clearly says we are all part of the same Body and each person belongs to the other. What impacts the well-being of my fellow Christian also impacts me as well.

For even as the body is one and yet has many members, and all the members of the body, though they are many, are one body, so also is Christ. (I Corinthians 12:12)

While this analogy is primarily used to refer to the variety of spiritual gifts, later in the same chapter, Paul broadens the application. "And if one member suffers, all the members suffer with it; if one member is honored, all the members rejoice with it" (I Corinthians 12:26).

91

Galatians 6:1-2 also tells us to restore anyone caught in a sin with "a spirit of gentleness." We can't help restore each other unless we are in some type of accountability relationship.

Besides the biblical principles that lead us to accountability, there is also my own personal experience and the testimony of the Body of Christ. Since I became a Christian thirty-seven years ago, godly Christians have been telling me about the importance of having a person to whom I am accountable.

When I went to a Whatever It Takes conference, I saw firsthand the damage a man's sin has on those he loves most. I saw men sharing their deepest, darkest secrets with their spouse in order to save their marriage. That's when the reality of Mark 10:7-9 hit me.

For this reason, a man shall leave his father and mother, and the two shall become one flesh; so they are no longer two, but one flesh. What therefore God has joined together, let no man separate.

The special relationship between a husband and wife is more intimate than any relationship except our relationship with God. While we associate Mark 10:9 with someone outside the relationship disrupting a marital union, the disruption can be caused by secret sins, especially when those sins are sexual in nature.

The reality of this separation became very real to me one day when I realized Satan was using a sexual fantasy that had bothered me since I was a teenager to make me feel guilty. My internal fears told me I could never tell my wife about it. Even though I had confessed it to God many times, the carnal thoughts would return. Satan had a foothold he could use anytime he wanted, all the while telling me I couldn't tell anyone about it.
One day, despite my reservations, I told my wife about the fantasy and told her I would tell her every time I was tempted to

have this fantasy. The next time the thoughts entered my mind, I immediately told her, and we prayed. Ever since that day, the fantasy has no longer been a struggle in my life. It's grip on me was my shame and my inability to be honest with my wife.

Despite Satan telling me there are some things you just have to keep to yourself, I learned there is something very powerful when you are transparent with your spouse. Rather than driving us apart, it has made us closer, and we have the shared confidence that our love is not based on the fairy tale of a being a perfect partner but on the unconditional love of one flawed human being for another.

The changes in our life have also been echoed through the life of my eldest son. Since he is single and does not have a spouse, he asked his mother and me to be his accountability partners for sexual temptations. This was not the first time he asked me to do so. When he was around fourteen years old, he tried to talk to me about struggles he was having. I deeply regret my reaction. I gave him a book and pointed him towards his youth minister at church. Not being there for my young son was one of my greatest failures. Years later, we have been able to develop a close relationship where my wife and I are able to share his struggles. It is not always easy for him or us. But it is one of the greatest honors we have ever had. Unfortunately, it has been made much more difficult since he has moved to another state.

When your family is not available to provide accountability, the church is another source of support. The apostle Paul even likens our relationships in the Body of Christ to the intimacy of family (Mark 10:7-9 and Ephesians 5:31-32).

Jesus is the Head of our spiritual family, and He is the first line of accountability.

If we confess our sins, He is faithful and righteous to forgive us our sins and to cleanse us from all unrighteousness. (1 John 1:9)

At the same time, it is also important to have flesh and blood accountability. Otherwise, why would James write, "Therefore, confess your sins to one another, and pray for one another so that you may be healed. The effective prayer of a righteous man can accomplish much" (James 5:16).

You absolutely need to be careful to whom you confess your failings. Your partner needs to be a mature believer whom you can trust to be compassionate and wise and someone who will maintain confidentiality. The scope of your confession also depends on the degree of your failure's impact. In rare cases, for example, when moral failure tarnishes the testimony of the whole congregation, confession is to be made to the church leadership with submission to their instruction and supervision.

In the book of Galatians, Paul tells the church:

Brethren, even if anyone is caught in any trespass, you who are spiritual, restore such a one in a spirit of gentleness; each one looking to yourself, so that you too will not be tempted. Bear one another's burdens, and thereby fulfill the law of Christ. For if anyone thinks he is something when he is nothing, he deceives himself. (Galatians 6:1-3)

Note that Paul tells us to bear one another's burdens. Paul then tells the Galatians:

But each one must examine his own work, and then he will have reason for boasting in regard to himself alone, and not in regard to another. For each one will bear his own load. (Galatians 6:4-5)

What is the difference? Why does Paul tell us to bear each other's burden only to turn around and tell us to carry our own load? Paul uses two different words for burden in Galatians 6. The word he uses in verse 5 is a specific word for a military pack. It is something every soldier is supposed to carry for himself. On the other hand, the burden in verses 1-3 refers to something too great for one person to carry on their own. Paul admonishes the church to help its members carry their trespass burdens, and he says if we don't, we are "nothing" and deceive ourselves if we think otherwise.

Just like the ancient fighters who relied on their neighbor to hold a shield over their head and parry unexpected blows, when we commit sin and confess to an accountability partner, either in our family or in our church, we are allowing someone to watch our back while we are fighting on the front lines with the consequences of our failure.

As important as having an accountability partner is, there are still dangers. Confession can be used to abuse the person being confessed to when the confession is made from impure motives or without a repentant heart. A minister recently told me about a woman who came up to him and said she wanted to confess she had hated him for a long time. Her confession was clearly intended to make her feel better without regard for the impact it would have on him. Until she made her confession, he had no idea there was a problem in their relationship. While there is a place for confession of animosity and grudges, it must come from brokenness, which takes full responsibility and is motivated by love and a need for reconciliation.

Another example of a person who abuses confessions is a person who uses them as a degrading and demoralizing weapon against someone, especially their partner. These confessions are frequently used to blame others for their own sinful choices and habits. "I slept with her because you ..." or "I drank too much because you ..."

In addition, when we use confession to an accountability partner as a substitute for going to the person or persons our moral failure has affected, we open the door for Satan's attack. A man I know went to one of his best friends to confess an affair he was having. Later, when his relationship with his best friend soured, the former friend threatened to break their promised confidentiality in order to punish him for perceived slights. It was emotional blackmail. Another man once came to me to confess he had embezzled a great deal of money seven years before. Since it was no longer possible for him to be charged with a crime, he wanted to confess his sin to someone so he could spend the money with a clear conscience. Accountability is never meant to be a substitute for repentance, reconciliation, and restitution.

Accountability relationships are most helpful when they shore up weaknesses in our life. The following are some questions one accountability partner might ask another:

How is your thought life going?

Have you been memorizing Scripture lately? Quote your memory verse.

Have you stuck to your diet this week?

Have you had quality time with your spouse this week?

Have you spent time alone with God every day this week?

Have you looked at anything you shouldn't have this week?

Have you controlled your temper this week?

Are you controlling your emotions, or are they controlling you?

Are you worrying about anything right now?

Have you used your time wisely this week?

What are you reading?

Have you read your Bible lately?

Have you abstained from _____ this week?

Have you spent time with your family this week?

What have you learned this week?

Have you walked through any boundaries this week?

Have you lied to me about anything this week?

Accountability partners meet regularly either in person or over the phone. They should have a preset list of agreed upon questions they ask each other, but they should also be able to pursue other topics if they feel it is necessary.

The second to the last question in the above list refers to boundaries. Boundaries are nonnegotiable limitations. Vice President Mike Pence received a great deal of grief because he said in an interview he would not dine alone with a woman who was not his wife. While many people condemned him as being a misogynist, this boundary is just common sense. Other boundaries might include:

Leaving the television off when alone.
Only surfing the Internet when others are able to see the screen.
Not traveling alone with a person of the opposite sex who is not your spouse.
Not flirting. Telling your spouse ASAP when someone flirts with you.
Not watching R or unrated movies.
Setting limitations on eating or drinking.
Turning off all electronics after a set time.

The nature of our boundaries is determined by the nature of our struggles. The Ministry of Failure includes the admission we cannot do anything we want and be the person God wants us to be. No matter how spiritual someone may be, there is weakness inherent in what the Bible calls our flesh. Intentionally setting boundaries so our flesh is not in control is an important part of spiritual warfare. It is protecting your weak flank from the attack of the enemy.

The battle of Gettysburg demonstrates the importance of protecting your weak flank. Colonel Chamberlin led the Twentieth Maine's bayonet charge down Little Round Top to stop the Confederate attack upon the Union army's flank. Colonel Chamberlin's men were virtually out of ammunition, and the enemy just kept attacking. The Twentieth Maine's audacious charge helped break the enemy's spirit and prevented the Confederate army from going around the flank to blindside the Union army's strength from the rear. There is nothing weak about protecting your weak flank. It is a sign of strength, wisdom, and determination.

From the beginning of our marriage, my wife and I set a boundary that we would not flirt with anyone else and if anyone flirted with us, we would immediately tell the other. I am at an age and weight now where flirting is not much of a problem. Early in my ministry, however, it was occasionally a concern.

I once received a call requesting counseling from a woman who visited our church. Since she asked me to come to her house, I verified that her husband would be there. I was surprised when he ignored the two of us as we went into the room next to where he was sitting. In the course of our conversation, she began flirting with me. I immediately excused myself and left the house. The woman followed me out to my car and, as I was leaving, leaned in and kissed me. I drove home as fast as I could and told my wife what had happened. The next Sunday there were half a dozen women ready to intercept this woman. Fortunately, she never came again.

The Culture of Success appeals to our pride: "I can handle it!"
The Ministry of Failure leads us to honestly admit, "No, I really can't!" and to set boundaries to protect ourselves from unnecessary failure.

I am the son of an alcoholic, and know the pull of alcohol on myself. I, therefore, set a boundary to abstain from alcohol. My drinking used to be frequent and heavy. I have only tasted alcohol twice in over thirty years—once on my honeymoon when my wife and I were mistakenly served vodka in our breakfast orange juice and once in the Lord's Supper at a church. I love being sober and wish more people would give up drinking. But imposing my boundary on other people who don't share my weakness and who choose to have a drink with friends or a beer with dinner, corrupts my boundary with judgmental pride, and my spiritual battle is close to being lost. Boundaries are an individual response to weakness and should not be imposed on others.

Pastors—the spiritual leaders of our churches—need accountability and boundaries as much or more than anyone else. Much of a pastor's ministry is about maintaining his testimony by living a holy life before everyone. When the appearance becomes more important than the reality, there is a problem. Remember, the holiest people in Jesus' day were Pharisees. It was to these people Jesus said, "For you are like whitewashed tombs which on the outside appear beautiful, but inside they are full of dead men's bones and all uncleanness" (Matthew 23:27).

Even in seminary, I remember an elderly professor stressing that pastors should never confess sins publicly before their congregation or use any church member as an accountability partner, because he must protect his appearance of holiness. Another of my seminary professors was old school even for thirty years ago. He admonished us to always wear a suit and tie in the pulpit in order to represent Christ well. He, for his part, admitted he never took off his suit and tie outside his house, even if he was mowing the grass, because he always wanted to be an example to everyone who saw him.

While I do not agree with these professors' approaches, I love their desire to do the right thing. A pastor must not be a person of gross immorality. Almost everyone knows stories about pastors who stepped over the line and had to leave ministry because of their sin. In Utah, a pastor whom I met with regularly—and thought I knew well—tried to treat the daughter of a church member like a prostitute. She went to her mother who then went to the church council. When confronted with his sin—which he did not deny—the pastor told the council what he did in his own personal time was no concern of the church. He was wrong. In the words of Jesus, "From everyone who has been given much, much will be required; and to whom they entrusted much, of him they will ask all the more" (Luke 12:48).

In the 1980s my wife and I moved from Texas to Florida. A few months before we left Texas, a preacher was caught up in a huge scandal. One of the most gifted and polished pastors in Texas destroyed his ministry when he was caught simultaneously having multiple extra-marital affairs. Imagine our shock when we arrived in Florida shortly afterward to see this pastor's image plastered on billboards announcing his new ministry in town. It is, unfortunately, all too easy for some pastors to live comfortably in the Culture of Success.

While pastors—especially those who try to live on a pedestal—have problems, they also tend to be the most "all in" group of men you will ever meet. As such, they also tend to be the ones with the most experience dealing with failure and should be the example in-chief. Accountable, yes. Perfect, no. Pastors can be the most powerful example of what it means to flesh out the Ministry of Failure. The more a pastor brings the struggles of real life into his sermons and peppers his Bible lessons with personal examples of failures and encounters with grace, the less likely the church will place the pastor on an unrealistic pedestal, and the more prepared his congregation will be to experience the same process.

Having spent a large part of my adult life either as a missionary or in between ministries, I have had the opportunity to sit under the teaching and leadership of some wonderful pastors. One pastor who has impacted me in a tremendous way is Joel Smith, a pastor in Mechanicsburg, Pennsylvania. Joel majored in communications in college and is a great speaker. But his speaking ability is not what has ministered to me most. Joel is the most transparent, authentic preacher I have ever heard. His willingness to open up about his struggles and faults has had a radical impact on the way I preach.

Besides being the example in-chief, it is also important for a pastor to have a person or a group of people within (and/or outside) the congregation who can be safely confided in. In some churches, these might be called elders. In other churches they might be called deacons or a pastor-staff relations committee. Whatever you call them, every pastor needs prayer support from people who have deep understanding of the Ministry of Failure and can have his back—one warrior standing next to another, holding up a shield of faith in prayer, fending off attacks of the enemy.

Finally, their role as example in-chief also means they can make a very effective accountability partner, especially for people within their direct realm of supervision. If a pastor is unable to serve a person effectively, for whatever reason, he should be available at the very least to serve as a referral and go-between for a person who is struggling and a person of high character and spiritual maturity who can serve as an accountability partner.

A Warrior's Shield and Armor—Our Faith Relationship with God

The second resource God has given us in our fight against moral failure is the shield and armor of our relationship with God.

In the ancient world, the quality of your armor frequently determined whether you made it through a battle in one piece or even at all. In some ways, our battle is more difficult than standing in a shield wall facing the Vikings or the Brits. Our enemy is invisible, powerful, and without mercy. It is important that we take the condition of our armor very seriously. According to Ephesians 6:10-17, our armor is made up of the girdle of truth, the breastplate of righteousness, the boots of the gospel of peace, the shield of faith, the helmet of our salvation, and the sword of the Spirit.

The girdle's purpose was to hold in the flowing robes of a warrior to make him better able to fight. Truth does the same thing in our life. Paul admonished the Corinthian church, "Do you not know

101

that those who run in a race all run, but only one receives the prize? Run in such a way that you may win" (I Corinthians 9:24). Whether fighting or running, it is difficult to win when you are tripped up by the extraneous. Truth tells us what we can (or need to) do without so we can focus our time and energy on the really important things of life. This may involve giving up a hobby, stopping a habit, or even changing careers.

The girdle of truth is also a powerful force in overcoming fear. Even animals know the comfort of being embraced. Our dog used to tremble during thunderstorms so badly that our entire bed shook when he put his paws up on the bed. Someone discovered that embracing a dog in a tight-fitting garment can give the animal a sense of security which helps prevent anxiety attacks during a thunderstorm. I am not sure why it works, but I have to believe the embrace of the girdle reminds some pets they live in their owner's security.

In 2 Timothy 1:7 we are told that God has not given us a fearful spirit but rather a spirit of "power and love and discipline." We cinch up the girdle of truth when we apply truth to our daily life, a process called discipleship. A discipler or discipleship leader is an experienced Christian who guides someone in this journey of discipline. When we are walking as Christ's disciples, we soon discover His power and love as He fulfills His promises in and to us. This focus on His power and love, instead of our inadequacy and failure, is crucial to overcoming fear and living a life of faith. "If His love can embrace and change me, then God can do anything," becomes our song of faith over our fears, including our fear of failure. Everyone struggles with fear at times. If you struggle with a recurring spirit of fear, you may want to seek out a discipleship relationship with someone who can guide you into the truth of who you are in Christ and who He is to you. As the prophet Isaiah said:

Behold, God is my salvation,
I will trust and not be afraid;

For the Lord God is my strength and song,
And He has become my salvation.
(Isaiah 12:2)

A friend and I were once driving through a major metropolitan city when we saw an obvious drug deal. I asked my friend to stop and call an ambulance if I needed one. When I walked over to the drug dealer, his customer freaked out and ran away. The drug dealer stood with cocaine smeared on his nose, proclaiming his innocence, obviously believing I was a policeman. I explained to him that I wasn't a policeman and began talking to him about what Jesus could do for him. The wonderful thing about the experience was the complete absence of fear. I felt overwhelming security in knowing I was doing what God wanted me to do. Considering I had once quit a night watchman job rather than confront drug dealers, the power of God's truth to overcome fear became very real to me. It is a lesson that must be relearned every time fear becomes a directional force in our life.

The next piece of our armor, the breastplate of a warrior, covers vital organs. The breastplate of righteousness in Christ is radically different than self-righteousness. Self-righteousness is looking down on other people because you believe yourself to be better than they are. The breastplate of righteousness is the rightness we graciously receive when we accept Jesus as our Savior and when we confess our moral failures. It was purchased by the sacrifice of Jesus and comes to us through the Ministry of Failure. Wearing it fills our heart with gratitude and love and protects the core of our spiritual life.

The gospel of peace is what keeps our feet moving forward in ministry. The word gospel means good news. The gospel is the good news of how God worked through the sacrifice of Jesus to bring us peace with Him, ourselves, and each other. Imagine a chasm dug by guilt and sin. We live at the bottom of that chasm. Triune God lives above it, perfect and holy, and yet is always present in the chasm. The Son of God enters our chasm by

103

indwelling human flesh in order to take the punishment for our guilt and shame. Because of His sacrifice, the Spirit of God can live within anyone who accepts Jesus as their Lord and Savior. God then teaches us to live together as His loving family, empowering us to bring this good news to other people in the chasm. At the same time, He gives us the assurance He will eventually draw us out of the chasm into His eternal presence. This is the gospel of peace.

The next piece of our armor is the shield of faith. In the ancient world, shields were often thick slabs of wood so flaming arrows would bury themselves in the wood and be extinguished by the lack of oxygen. We have been offered the shield of faith to protect us against Satan's attempts to destroy us through fiery trials. Faith does this largely by changing a person's worldview. How you view the difficulties and trials of life is strongly affected by your faith perspective.

A Hindu co-worker once told me he hated life because there was no point to the trials he experienced. He knew he would never be good enough to break the cycle of reincarnation, and his religion offered him no other way. Christianity, on the other hand, takes an honest look at the fiery arrows of the enemy and snuffs out their fire through a simple reality: "And we know that God causes all things to work together for good to those who love God, to those who are called according to His purpose" (Romans 8:28). Satan's arrows may still cause damage and pain, but faith gives us the assurance their effect is ultimately to the glory of God.

The last piece of the armor is the helmet, which protected a person's head and brain. It is a picture of how our salvation changes the way we think and the way we view life. It is a good thing it does. God does not think like we think. His thoughts are not our thoughts. In fact, Paul says "the wisdom of this world is foolishness before God" (I Corinthians 3:19).

In the musical Fiddler on the Roof there is a wonderful song called "If I Were a Rich Man." In this song, a poor man, Tevye, dreams of being rich. If he were wealthy, other men would come to him for the answers to difficult questions. He believes it wouldn't matter if he answers right or wrong, because people think you have all the answers when you are rich. The truth is, it doesn't matter how rich we are. Only God knows the answers to the truly difficult questions. Only God knows why we are the way we are. Only God knows why we have failed. Only God knows what we need to do to be successful and be the person He intends for us to be.

If we are ever to be truly successful (according to God's definition of success) God's thoughts need to become our thoughts. Unfortunately, God's ways are so foreign to us it is a waste of time to try to imagine what He might think. The scribes and Pharisees, for example, were the most respected wise men of their day, and they completely missed the mind of God when it came to the Nazarene carpenter. The fact that we are unable to trust our own understanding brings us to the third resource in overcoming failure, the Word of God.

A Warrior's Weapon – God's Word

The image Paul gives us of the Bible is a sword. A sword is primarily an offensive weapon, but it is also an important source of protection as it wards off the attacks of the enemy. Reading the Bible is the first step in discovering principles to live by which will help you avoid moral failures. I have always recommended that people who are starting off on their first adventure exploring the Bible should begin by reading either the book of Mark or the book of Luke. Both are powerful, easy to read testimonies of Jesus and His ministry.

Once you begin reading the Bible, you will naturally want to get to know it better. Studying the Bible, memorizing Scriptures (especially ones about victory over specific areas of failure),

105

thinking about what you have learned, listening to what others have learned, and obeying its truths are all important ways God can do a deep work in your life, changing you so you no longer repeat failures that are so destructive.

When I became a Christian at the age of nineteen, I knew very little about the Bible. I had been exposed to many of the stories as a child in Sunday school, but outside of that, had read very little of it. In fact, when my new pastor said, "And John 3:16 says ... oh, you know what it says," and failed to read the verse, I went home to look up the verse to discover, "For God so loved the world, that He gave His only begotten Son, that whoever believes in Him shall not perish, but have eternal life." I remember thinking how wonderful this verse is.

The first Bible verse I ever memorized was Matthew 6:33. It was easy to memorize, because we sang it as a chorus almost every Sunday at our church. One day, while in college, I took a bus from my college campus to a parking lot where my aunt's old, worn-out 1964 Oldsmobile was waiting to take me home to my grandmother's house. Just as I got off the bus, another college student drove by in an unbelievably expensive sports car. I instantaneously wondered why he got that car and I had to drive a junker. The words of Matthew 6:33 responded by immediately popping into my head.

I thought about the verse all the way home. When I got home, I turned on the radio in my room and plopped down on my bed to read my Bible. At the time, I didn't know the difference, so I always opened the Bible to wherever it naturally opened and began reading. This time my Bible opened to Matthew, chapter 5. I read on until, as I got to Matthew 6:33, a song came on the radio: "Seek ye first the kingdom of God and His righteousness and all these things shall be added unto you" (KJV).

I read these words exactly as they were proclaimed through my radio. God could not have shouted, "Forget the car and focus on

106

what is important!" any louder if He had sent an angel into my bedroom.

While God seldom shouts His Word at us, He does use His Word to direct the desires of our heart. Psalm 119:9 says, "How can a young man keep his way pure? By keeping it according to Your Word." When we meditate on and memorize the Bible, we allow God to provide us with guidance which can protect us from failure.

As you develop the habit of meditation and memorization, you might want to consider beginning with the following Scriptures. Set your mind on the things above, not on the things that are on earth. (Colossians 3:2)

All have sinned and fall short of the glory of God. (Romans 3:23) For God so loved the world, that He gave His only begotten Son, that whoever believes in Him shall not perish, but have eternal life. (John 3:16)

If we confess our sins, He is faithful and righteous to forgive us our sins and to cleanse us from all unrighteousness. (I John 1:9) For My thoughts are not your thoughts, nor are your ways My ways, declares the Lord. (Isaiah 55:8)

Be kind to one another, tender-hearted, forgiving each other, just as God in Christ also has forgiven you. (Ephesians 4:32)

For I know the plans that I have for you, declares the Lord, plans for welfare and not for calamity to give you a future and a hope. (Jeremiah 29:11)

Treat others the same way you want them to treat you. (Luke 6:31)

Trust in the Lord with all your heart, and do not lean on your own understanding. (Proverbs 3:5)

When I am afraid, I will put my trust in You. (Psalms 56:3)
I can do all things through Him who strengthens me. (Philippians 4:13)

Your Word I have treasured in my heart, that I may not sin against You. (Psalm 119:11)

And we know that God causes all things to work together for good to those who love God, to those who are called according to His purpose. (Romans 8:28)

Therefore, if anyone is in Christ, he is a new creature; the old things passed away; behold, new things have come. (2 Corinthians 5:17)

All of these verses are taken from the New American Standard Version. Whatever version you are comfortable with is the version you memorize from. It is also good to memorize the reference so you know where to find the verse later.

Besides reading, memorization, and meditation, God also sharpens our attack against our spiritual enemy through regular Bible study.

I went through a period of time in my life when I was under personal stress, causing me to have difficulty breathing. I do not know why this became an issue in my life, but my wife always knew when I was feeling stressed out because I yawned frequently, trying to draw in enough oxygen. It was a miserable feeling, and I desperately wanted to find a way to calm my needless worries.

Anxiety's hold on me was finally broken through personal Bible studies on the nature of God's faithfulness. These studies filled my mind with verses like Hebrews 13:5: "I will never desert you, nor will I ever forsake you." I found it was impossible to dwell on verses like this and still worry.

Cynthia Bills is a woman who also struggled with anxiety. She grew up with an alcoholic father and a critical, suicidal mother. From a young age, she learned that her security and emotional survival depended upon her earning her demanding father's acceptance. Her extended family did little to help. Family gatherings were characterized by excessive drinking, smoking, dirty jokes, bigoted comments, cursing, and verbal sparring. As an only child, she grew up with an acute awareness that she did not fit in. In college, she joined a Christian fellowship group and a good church where she began to grow spiritually. She also met a wonderful Christian man whom she married.

Approximately ten years and three children later, I was drowning in a sea of anxiety. I found that I could never be a good enough mother, and the leaders in our church at the time were very quick to tell me that I was too sensitive. I attended a seminar on anxiety and was told that what I needed to do was to discipline my thoughts and focus on God rather than on my fears. My attempts to comply only exacerbated the anxiety problem, but again, the Lord provided help, this time in the form of a gifted Christian counselor.

Over the course of two years, I began to understand the messages I had received as a child and how I used those messages to draw conclusions about who God is, who I am, and who I am before Him. And, thus, started a long journey that is not yet complete. As a Christian counselor myself now, I recognize the lies I have internalized, and I continue to work in cooperation with the Holy Spirit to reject them and embrace the Lord's gracious truth. Some days are better than others. It is still easy for me to serve the opinions and expectations of others, or worse yet, myself. I am often tempted to take responsibility that isn't mine. But I can now say that while the anxiety "noose" remains on my shoulders, it is loose enough for me to breathe deeply. And the reminder of its presence keeps me deeply and gratefully dependent on my Lord and Redeemer.

Cindy has shared with me that anxiety makes experiencing God's goodness in failure especially difficult because of the perceived association between failure and rejection. Even people who don't suffer from anxiety frequently struggle with the stigma of failure since our culture defines success according to performance. Moving beyond personal self-deceptions, including unrealistic expectations, perfectionism, and fear of failure and/or rejection, in order to experience God in failure often requires a transformation in our thinking.

Learning more about God through the Bible is a crucial part of replacing the lies we have told ourselves with the truth. For the technologically savvy, there are wonderful online resources such as Biblegateway.com and Navigators.com which can help us explore, study, and experience the powerful truths of God's Word.

This process of internalizing and understanding God's Word is an important element in a lifetime journey of discovery. It is a journey that can be painful at times. Hebrews 4:12 describes the Bible as "sharper than any two-edged sword" and says that it pierces us "as far as the division of soul and spirit." We are undergoing nothing less than spiritual surgery when our long-held beliefs are confronted with truth.

Like many men, I was confronted with the truth that I wasn't eighteen as I tried to recapture my youthful body while in middle age. My rotator cuff tore while I was in the middle of a bench press, requiring surgery. After the anesthesia wore off, I awoke to the reality that healing can be the most painful part of surgery. The same is sometimes true of spiritual surgery. When the Bible reveals our spiritual and emotional misconceptions, healing comes from being painfully honest with ourselves, God, and others. A humble, teachable spirit is crucial if we are to experience the freedom of becoming the person we are meant to be.

A young man we have known for many years joined the military and did not like the way he was treated when he arrived in boot camp. From the moment they yelled in his face, he was done. He went into the military with the same rebellious spirit and stubbornness which had virtually destroyed his civilian life. After about a week, he was thrown into the brig where he stayed until boot camp was over.

If our heart has not been broken and humbled by the Ministry of Failure, the girdle of truth, the breastplate of righteousness, the boots of the gospel of peace, the shield of faith, the helmet of salvation, and the sword of the Spirit are impossible to put on and carry. At the same time, if we are honest with ourselves and see our limitations, this armor is crucial in developing true success.

Conspicuously missing in this chapter is the important role prayer plays in our lives. Prayer undergirds everything we do. Paul tells us to "pray without ceasing" (I Thessalonians 5:17). It is how we begin our journey with God and how we put on the armor of God every day. As we spend time in God's Word and God speaks to our heart, it is only natural to respond in prayer. As we fight spiritual battles through the day, it is only natural to call on our Commander in Chief for direction and assistance. As we experience God's goodness and blessings, it is only natural to rejoice in thanksgiving.

Shy Lawing and her husband built a successful trucking company. Life was good until Shy was devastated by the death of her father, followed a few months later by the discovery that her husband was having an affair. Subsequent attempts to control her share of the company she helped build were tied up in court until she could no longer afford to pay legal bills. Two subsequent businesses she started failed and she ended up losing her house which she had worked hard to purchase on her own.

While some people turn everything they touch into gold, it began to seem like everything I touched turned to coal. I felt like I had lost everything. I began feeling suicidal, hopeless and helpless. My kids were just eleven and six and the responsibility of failing my kids was overwhelming. There were times my dinner was a piece of fruit so my kids could eat better meals. I prayed and I felt like God just wasn't hearing me. But God put a sense in my spirit that this was my boot camp. I didn't want to hear that. I just wanted things to be right. I wasn't trying to go through some kind of spiritual exercise...

But I did begin reconnecting spiritually. I started spending more time than I ever did with God. Throughout the day it was constant. I didn't do a lot of talking with people. I stayed in my head a lot. I stayed in prayer in my mind. Not necessarily praying out loud, but just talking to God throughout my day which was something new for me. Of course you have your morning prayer, your night prayer, but I was constantly praying. I just wanted to be in His will so bad that I just couldn't break away. Whenever I was at work, whatever I was doing, I would have sermons playing in the background. I just had something constantly going on that was spiritually uplifting. During my lunch breaks I would take walks and I would pray. During other breaks I would pull out my Bible. It was all God.

My circumstances had not changed. There still was no hope and everything was gone. At the same time, I started to have faith and trust again. I always thought that I could get myself out of tough situations and that I was resourceful and could make it happen. Then God broke me down to my lowest point and showed me that the blessings in my life had nothing to do with me and were all Him and because of Him. He had to get me to that point for me to understand that I had nothing to do with it.

112

Once I got to that point, I was okay. I had nothing but peace. People would express their sympathy and leave thinking I was crazy. "Oh, my, she's gone!" They didn't know that I had this inner peace and everything was fine. I didn't have a house and I had a terrible job but I was fine.

After Shy found her peace in God, her circumstances began to miraculously change. She is now a successful counselor and consultant. I asked her what she learned through her experiences.

Through everything I have learned how important it is to trust God. Trials aren't a death sentence. Instead they can be a catapult to victory. When you are going through the pain, sometimes all you can see is the pain but if you look hard you can see God at the other end of the tunnel. He is going to give us everything we need to get through it. If you focus on your problem then that is all you see. If you focus on God, that is all you see.

God brought me back to why we read His word. I had to ask myself if I was reading the Bible to just read it or if I was internalizing it so that it could became part of who I really am. The truths of the Bible are God trying to give us a directive for life because He knows that we are going to go through these challenges. He wants us to know what to do when we are going through them.

Losing everything was hard.. It taught me how strong I am in Him. I could not have imagined that I could have survived something like that. Because of what I went through I now know that there is nothing that I cannot overcome with Him. It made me a different person. I didn't enjoy the pain but now I really know who I am. I am a warrior who can do all things through Christ who strengthens me.

Is it possible that where we see a dead end, God sees detours? When we see ourselves at the bottom of the barrel, does God see an opportunity to start over again on a better path? Where we see an enemy, does God see an opportunity to love? Where we see complete failure, could God see an opportunity for forgiveness and restoration? We tend to define our life by our success or failure. Prayer, combined with Bible reading and a teachable spirit, provides God an important opportunity to help us see our life as He sees it.

Robert Frost's poem "A Passing Glimpse" says, "Heaven gives its glimpses only to those not in position to look too close." In other words, beauty is often found in divinely inspired fleeting moments of truth. Elijah was a hunted man, hiding in a cave from people who wanted to kill him. He longed to die. Then the wind outside his cave began to blow fiercely, the earth shook, and the hill burst into fire. That would have been enough to drive me out of the cave. Who wants to be in a cave during an earthquake or when the smoke from a forest fire is pouring in? But Elijah stayed hunkered down. It wasn't until he heard the gentle voice of God that he was able to leave his hidey hole and find his path to success.

In his conversation with God, Elijah said, "I alone am left; and they seek my life, to take it away" (I Kings 19:14). In response, God give Elijah instructions for his next steps and encouraged him that he was not alone. There were other people who could support him and whom he could support.

My son recently became a captain in the Marines. It is amazing the change which has occurred in him as he has become a warrior. Through personal accountability, focusing on developing our spiritual life, getting the support of other warriors, obeying biblical principles and communicating with God, we can become the spiritual warriors God wants us to be. Hiding in the cave of our failure—it's just the way I am—as an excuse for failure has no place in the Christian life. If the Ministry of Failure teaches anything, it is that God is not done with us yet. Listen for God's quiet encouragement. Look for people who can support you and whom you can support. Get out of your cave and fight the fight before you.

Sherise's Story

My husband Mark and I had been friends since college. I was a freshman nursing student and Mark was a junior studying finance. We were both young Christians. After marriage, we became faithfully involved in several ministries. Mark became a deacon in our local church. Young and struggling couples came to us for advice and, to others, we appeared to be the model family.

One Friday afternoon, my husband called home and asked if we could talk together later that night. I suggested we sit down over coffee at a small diner near the building where our daughter took gymnastics lessons. He agreed. Our evening plans made, I hung up the phone, thinking little of what had just passed.

That night, as we sipped coffee and sampled some desserts, our conversation abruptly turned from casual chit-chat to heart-wrenching confession. The gist of it was this: In twenty-five minutes, my husband of almost twenty-five years slowly and painstakingly admitted to being involved in an extramarital relationship at work.

At the time, what he said made no sense to me. Over the years we had been married, Mark and I had never had any major disagreements, but, looking back, our relationship was hollow. We were both very busy. In the whirlwind of children, careers, and church, it sometimes felt as though we were living parallel lives—moving in the same direction without ever intersecting.

When Mark began to travel more for his job, stress-lines started to show. We knew that things could be better. We made small attempts to improve our relationship, but we were only addressing the outward symptoms.

During one such difficult season, and after a particularly tense dinner with Mark, I remember praying, "God, I can at least thank you for giving me a faithful husband." Not only was my relationship with my husband quickly cooling, but it was founded on misinformation. I believed he was being faithful, but he was involved with another woman. What began as inappropriate thoughts, then innocent flirtations, eventually grew to fantasy and, finally, sexual encounters during business trips. I learned the hard way you can't put your trust in anyone.

As Mark began to confess his secret relationship to me in the diner that night, overwhelming thoughts rushed through my mind. Though I felt hurt and ashamed, I needed to know the exact details of everything he had done. I needed to paint a picture in my mind of what had really happened. I thought of my three children. I would not—could not—put them through a painful divorce. My childhood home had been shattered in just such a way, and I refused to relive history. I also thought of the vows Mark and I had exchanged on our wedding day. Did we really intend to work it all out, "for better or for worse?"

My life skidded to an abrupt stop that moment in the diner. Nothing I had trusted was real. What I thought had been twenty-five years of normal, healthy marriage now looked like twenty-five years of heartbreak in the making. As I sat across from Mark, I searched his face for something to hold on to, some sign of hope. Mark was there, looking back at me, probably straining to catch a glimpse of the same in my eyes. We found nothing that night, and only left the diner when it started getting late. The drive back home was very dark and very quiet.

Over the next several weeks, sometimes late into the night, I would ask questions about the details of their relationship until Mark answered me. My mind was flooded with lies and fears. I needed the truth. Even though it was painful, once the details—

including the lies, deception, and hidden sins—were exposed, I felt a certain temporary relief.

Slowly, I learned to go about my daily routines again. Life was normal. Normal, that is, in the sense that I was forced to redefine normal every moment of each new day. Underneath its functional exterior, my world was upside down. I could no longer trust the person I once considered to be my best friend, lover, and protector. Even worse, I found myself growing distant from friends. Given the way things stood between Mark and myself, I was afraid to let other people uncover our shame and embarrassment. I found it difficult to pray and was unsettled by how easily I avoided spiritual activities. God was shut out too.

Fortunately, God always has a way of letting Himself back in, even when we try our hardest to keep the door shut. It was around this time I first heard Him speak to me about forgiveness. In not so subtle ways, God made it clear I needed to forgive my husband before He could begin working on Mark's dull heart. At first, I strongly objected. I asked God, "What about me?" After all, Mark is the one who failed. I was the one who had been hurt, not Mark. But every time I questioned God's commandment to forgive, He reminded me that Mark and I are both His children. His plan was for both of us. Any grudges between us would only get in the way. When I finally humbled myself enough to step aside, God started to move in powerful ways.

Through the process of forgiving Mark, I was able to gradually overcome all my shock, denial, and anger. God gave me the courage I needed to face Mark's sin, then He gave me the grace I needed to forgive it all. As my husband confessed his wrongdoings and I forgave them, I was surprised to see God do marvelous work in my own heart. The act of forgiveness humbled me. I realized, in light of what Jesus accomplished on the cross, I was just as much of a sinner as Mark was. I began to ask Mark to forgive me for times I had wronged him in our relationship over the years. God had never forgotten me. I was just as much His child as Mark was, and forgiveness was His way of healing us both.

During the next several months, Mark and I had to relearn our marriage. We were afraid of reverting back to the typical interactions which had characterized our last twenty-five years together. Because our hurts were so fresh and painful, we had to take things slowly. We first tried to be more honest and open with each other. However, at the same time, I really wasn't feeling safe. In fact, I felt very vulnerable. Based upon our individual struggles and weaknesses, we began establishing boundaries—understanding certain occasions could easily trigger harmful thoughts and behaviors.

Mostly, we played and prayed together like never before. In all honesty, though, we were still teaching each other the steps to an unfamiliar dance, and at first it was very awkward.

It was tempting to rush ahead. I just wanted to get to the other side of reconciliation where there would be hope, healing, and peace. I wanted a little bit of normal. More than anything else, I wanted to trust Mark again. But God held me back. He made me realize I was putting—that I had always been putting—my trust in the wrong place. Ever since my father abandoned me when I was very young, I had been seeking to fill that void where a trusting relationship should have been. At first, I tried to put my stepfather there, but he not-so-subtly hinted he wanted no part of me. As a teen, I began to crave the trust and security of a romantic relationship, and I eventually found Mark. For over twenty-five years, I had worked to build my own safe little world centered around my marriage. Overnight, my trust was broken, and my foundation vanished.

Now, the Lord showed me how misguided I had been all along. When I had tried to fill that void with Mark, I had staked all my hopes and dreams on a sinner who was doomed to fail. I had placed an impossible burden on my husband's shoulders. My

118

trust should have been in Christ and Him alone. He is capable of carrying every burden we bring to Him. I would never have peace until I learned to entrust my welfare—and Mark's welfare—to His care.

When I first started to trust God and release my death-grip on Mark, I had no guarantees Mark would stay faithful to me. The only thing that gave me peace as I let go was God's guarantee He would be with me and never fail me. However, there was one nagging concern I could not easily dismiss: Now that I was no longer going to put my trust in Mark, what was I to expect of him? I felt like I was in limbo, and I struggled to find a foundation for our life together. I remember asking a friend in whom I had confided, "When will I have peace again?"

Soon after my decision to trust God in all things, Mark and I attended a Whatever It Takes (WIT) marriage intensive together. Other Christian couples who had survived the pain of a broken marriage ministered to Mark and me in an open and compassionate environment. We walked away from the weekend feeling better equipped to work together towards healing. I had a better understanding of what a healthy marriage should look like. If Mark and I could learn to see each other for what we really were—fellow sinners walking the same road together—and live humbly in the light of Christ's sacrificial love, we would grow together as one spirit. I knew that was all I could expect of Mark and all he could want from me.

Through all this, God showed me if I wanted to flourish as a wife, I first needed to flourish as His child. My hope and trust had to be in Christ and no one else. Then, and only then, could I have confidence in my husband as our mutual love for Christ spilled over into our love for one another. Because I could trust what God was doing in my husband's heart, I could trust Mark's growing desire to cherish and protect me. It has now been several years since that night in the diner when my husband and I (though we did not know it at the time) began our journey towards healing.

We are still awestruck by God's grace and the way in which He took our broken marriage and made it whole, restoring our relationship to a condition more beautiful than it was before. True, Mark and I do bear emotional scars which remind us of how bad things used to be. Yet those same scars are proof God works miracles. After all, He found us in our sorrowful state, showed Himself to be the solution to our sins, and now calls us to share with others the hope and freedom only found by placing all our trust in Him.

Author's Note: There are many lessons to be learned from Sherise's story, including the use of boundaries. These boundaries were designed to provide Sherise confidence and safety. They also protected Mark's "weak flank" while he rediscovered his freedom in Christ. While Mark may have initially struggled to explain his changed behavior to other people, these boundaries became a personal expression of love for his wife.

Meditation Moment

- Is there a person in your life you can trust to be an accountability partner? How would you go about enlisting their support? What guidelines would you want to establish in order to begin a healthy accountability relationship? What areas in your life would you want to address with accountability questions?

- Do you have any boundaries already set up in your life? What boundaries could you set up which would improve the quality of your relationship with God or with other people? In I Corinthians 8:13, Paul says, "Therefore, if food causes my brother to stumble, I will never eat meat again, so that I will not cause my brother to stumble." Are their behaviors in your life which might make someone else stumble? Are you willing to protect others by setting limitations on your own freedom?

- "For My thoughts are not your thoughts, nor are your ways My ways," declares the Lord (Isaiah 55:8). What does this verse tell you about your way of thinking about yourself and your failures? Is there a verse in chapter seven which helps you see failure from God's perspective?

- This chapter describes briefly the girdle of truth, the breastplate of righteousness, the boots of the gospel of peace, the shield of faith, the helmet of our salvation, and the sword of the Spirit. Overcoming failures can be a real struggle. Are their areas in your life you need to remove to stop yourself from stumbling? Are you willing to face these struggles with God's armor and God's word empowered by the Spirit of God through prayer?

Chapter Seven

Sharpening the Ax

The greatest blessing is learning something about my shortcomings I need to work on.

Putting on the full armor of God, having an accountability partner, and filling your mind with biblical truth are all needed in order to avoid and overcome failure. As important as these are, there are additional, powerful resources God has given us to prevent unnecessary failure.

This book has focused on lessons learned from my failures. This is probably appropriate given the book's topic. At the same time, God would not be getting full credit if I did not admit I have had some wonderful successes. I say this realizing I cannot guarantee success any more than I can control failure. Success always comes by the grace of God. There are, nonetheless, certain patterns we can develop which God can use to prepare us for success.

Two short years after I became a Christian, God called me into Christian ministry. My initial reaction was to be overwhelmed and, for a brief time, I emotionally ran from God. Once I finally reached the point of surrender, I made an appointment with my pastor to discuss my next steps. He immediately told me to go to seminary, something that didn't interest me at all. His argument was persuasive. He said, "Two men go into a forest to chop wood. Both men work equally hard. One has a sharpened ax, and the other has a dull ax. Which is going to be more successful?"

While most people are not called to go to seminary (many people have been very successful without advanced degrees), few have been successful without taking time to prepare themselves in some way for their chosen endeavors. This reality is especially pertinent to followers of Jesus, since we never know what adventure God may have for us next. If you are following your own life agenda, you may be comfortable in the status quo. If you are obeying someone else who has absolute authority over every aspect of your life, it is important you place a value on constantly learning.

As a math teacher, I realize many students feel math is irrelevant to their lives. Their lack of appreciation for algebra, geometry and trigonometry is frequently expressed and is not entirely their fault. Anyone who has seen the lame word problems in most algebra books understands why someone would question the day-to-day application of the subject. "A farmer has a rectangular field whose sides are $x + 4$ and $3x - 5$. If the farmer's field is 139 square feet and the field is twice as long as it is wide, what are the approximate dimensions of the field?"

In response to their objections to questions like this, I tell my students they are learning to think, and they have no idea what they might find themselves doing one day. To emphasize my point, I often recount a breakfast I had with a plumber and an electrician. When these men found out I was teaching geometry, their reaction surprised and encouraged me. Both men said, "At least you are teaching your students something practical they can use every day." Learning is never a waste of time.

Like many young couples, my wife and I had very little when we married. Our dining table was a folding card table. That table and the four folding chairs with it, together with my bedroom furniture from my high school days and some living room furniture passed down by my in-laws, was the extent of our furniture. We had very little and we were happy.

Since I was almost finished earning my degree, and my future father-in-law had made me promise his daughter could finish her education before we moved anywhere, I decided to reduce my class load and begin working full time. For the first time in our lives we had a decent cash flow. And for the first time in our lives we found ourselves in conflict over money. We learned the hard way the truth of a quote attributed to John D. Rockefeller. The story goes that he was asked, "How much money is enough?" Rockefeller answered, "Just a little bit more!"

Fortunately, at this same time our church offered a financial management course. The principles of budgeting and stewardship learned through this class have changed our lives. While my salary has fluctuated radically over the years of our marriage, I can honestly say the only times we have had financial stress in our relationship were the two times we thought we were ready to stop keeping a budget. It didn't take long to realize we needed to get back to the financial basics we had learned through that church course.

Preventing failure and overcoming failure both involve either learning new principles or applying previously learned principles which have been neglected. These principles are readily available through Christian and secular books, books on tape, church discipleship courses, online courses, and courses offered through local schools. Whatever avenue of learning we choose, it is important to develop a mindset that says "God is not done with me yet. I need to be prepared." A friend of our family earned his master's degree in counseling at the age of eighty. At the time of the writing of this book, he is ninety-nine years old and still studying new ballroom dance steps. He is a man who has taken this mindset and built a lifetime around it.

A single person sharpens his or her ax when they spend time reading about building strong relationships and marriages. A single mother sharpens her ax when she takes time to participate in a church course on intercessory prayer so she can more effectively pray for her children. Focusonthefamily.com offers many resources which can help every parent sharpen important parenting skills. Books and seminars by Dave Ramsey provide principles which can help any family sharpen their financial ax.

We live in a time of incredible technological change. My ninety-nine-year-old friend remembers sneaking into black-and-white silent movies as a child. My father remembered the first television set on his block. I remember as a child sitting amazed in front of our small black-and-white television watching Neil Armstrong walk on the moon. By the time I was in college, the same computing power that guided Armstrong's ship to the moon was available to everyone through home computers. Today's generations have seen the advent of self-driving cars and the outer space tourist industry.

Technology is neither moral nor immoral, but it can be dangerous. Ignoring it and failing to learn to utilize it is a recipe for failure in many careers. At the same time, becoming so dependent on it that you fail to strengthen your own brain is a serious and growing problem.

When I first entered teaching, we were taught the human brain was able to grow and learn new thought patterns until young adulthood. At that point, we were kind of stuck with whatever intellectual ability we had. Recent research has changed our understanding of how the brain works. In 2008, for example, professors at the University of Bern published an important study which changed the way many people look at intelligence. Their study demonstrated we can improve our ability to learn by exposing ourselves to new learning opportunities.[12]

We literally become smarter every time we train our brain to master new information and skills. It doesn't matter how old you are or what educational struggles you have had in the past, lifelong learning is a crucial part of God sharpening our ax, preparing us to be more successful and to overcome failures in our life.

Another way we sharpen our ax is through the influence of others. Proverbs 27:17 says, "Iron sharpens iron, so one man sharpens another." There are two ways one person sharpens another person: irritation and inspiration. Irritation is probably the most direct application of this verse. Specifically, when two iron implements are brought together, it is the roughness of one that knocks off the rough edges of the other and sharpens it.

Every time I feel irritated with someone, it is an indication there is an area of my life which needs to be developed. Irritation with another person is frequently a sign of impatience, condescension, a lack of information, a lack of love, prejudice, pride, and/or misplaced priorities. If I respond to irritation by blaming the other person, I open myself up to failure by responding in a destructive way. But if I respond to irritation by examining honestly the source of the irritation in my own life, I can adjust my attitude and respond appropriately. While it is often challenging in the heat of the moment to bite our tongue while we adjust our attitude, it is also crucial. Sometimes the most spiritual thing we can do is to take time to consider and choose the wisest reaction in difficult situations.

I work in an inner-city school with a high tolerance for behaviors not allowed in most other schools. In addition, our school district does not have sufficient alternative programs available for students who do not have the temperament or behavioral skills to be successful in the classroom. As a result, I have numerous students in my classes who pose severe behavioral problems. While many of them do not come to school at all, a few make a point of coming almost every day and can be an extreme source of disruption. I currently have several of these students in the same class, and I have found myself severely irritated every day.

As I prayed about my attitude and my growing sense of anger towards these youth, God told me the problem was within myself. I could not change the school district or the school's policies, but I could learn to love these students. The day after

126

God said this to me, another student walked by my most challenging student and playfully tapped him on the head. I saw an opportunity and immediately rebuked the offender saying, "Don't touch my man." Another student saw the interaction and was stunned. He said, "How can you say that after the way he acts and what he says to you?" I simply affirmed this young man was important to me and moved on.

The change in this challenging student was almost instantaneous. He was still defiant and unproductive as a student, but he was no longer confrontational. The greatest blessing of all to me was learning something about my shortcomings that need work.

The second way people can help sharpen our ax is through inspiration. The classic illustration of this in the Bible is Moses and his father-in-law Jethro. If there was ever a leader set up for failure, it was Moses. God had used Moses in a miraculous way to lead the children of Israel out of slavery and into the wilderness. Now that they were in the wilderness, Moses was their spiritual, political, legal, and cultural leader all rolled up into one.

When Jethro brought Moses' family to him, he found Moses holding court every day as people by the thousands tried to get a hearing before him. Jethro told Moses, "The thing that you are doing is not good. You will surely wear out, both yourself and these people who are with you, for the task is too heavy for you; you cannot do it alone" (Exodus 18:17-18). He told Moses how responsibilities could be divided among leaders in each of the tribes of Israel so the burden would not be too great on any one person. Fortunately for Moses (and everyone else), he was wise enough to listen to this counsel.

Everyone needs wise people in their life whom they can use as sounding boards when life is challenging. As Proverbs 11:14 says, "Where there is no guidance the people fall, but in abundance of counselors there is victory." My wife is a

127

professional counselor, and I have spent many hours counseling people as their pastor. We both have people in our life we look to for advice when we are struggling. My wife also has a group of other counselors she meets with monthly to discuss issues related to her work and to support each other.

Whether you turn to a parent, a friend, a pastor, a support group, a professional counselor, or a leader in your chosen field, it is important—if you don't want to fall—to have an abundance of counselors and weigh their advice carefully. If you decide you want to locate a professional counselor in your area, the American Association of Christian Counselors offers a search engine that can help you identify counselors across the entire United States. Familylife.com and ccn.thedirectorywidget.com (a website developed by Focus on the Family) also provide lists of state, local, and national counselors and counseling organizations.

When Solomon died, his son Rehoboam became king in his place. Immediately after taking the throne, Rehoboam was visited by leaders from the northern ten tribes. They told him if he would lighten the heavy load his father Solomon had placed on them they would serve him the rest of their lives. Two groups counseled Rehoboam. The elders who had served his father encouraged him to respond positively to the request for leniency. Rehoboam's friends who he grew up with in the royal court gave him radically different advice.

When the leaders returned, Rehoboam followed the advice of his friends and said, "My little finger is thicker than my father's loins! Whereas my father loaded you with a heavy yoke, I will add to your yoke; my father disciplined you with whips, but I will discipline you with scorpions" (I Kings 12:10-11). Needless to say, this response was not well received. As a result of Rehoboam's foolishness, the nation split as the northern tribes broke off.

I am not stretching the message of this story much when I point out the fact that we don't seek the counsel of our senior adults enough in our culture. Proverbs 4:1 says, "Hear, O sons, the instruction of a father, and give attention that you may gain understanding." At what age do we stop listening? Being old doesn't necessarily make a person wise, but there is a perspective that comes from passing years which comes no other way. Perhaps this is the reason why leaders in the early church were called elders. I am personally very thankful for my mother and father-in-law and the wisdom they have given us over the years.

Of course, one way elders in our church inspire us is through their sermons. Paul told Timothy, "Preach the word; be ready in season and out of season; reprove, rebuke, exhort, with great patience and instruction" (2 Timothy 4:2). My father-in-law describes preaching as a form of group counseling. It is a wonderful way of addressing everyday issues and truths which impact everyone.

While it is impossible for every sermon to directly address the needs and concerns of every person listening, it is amazing how many times people have told me a sermon spoke to them about areas in their life unrelated to the sermon topic. This phenomenon is as old as preaching itself. Paul said, "which things we also speak, not in words taught by human wisdom, but in those taught by the Spirit, combining spiritual thoughts with spiritual words" (1 Corinthians 2:13).

A popular preacher once took a camera crew to the houses of some of his church leaders on Monday evening, asking them what the sermon was about the day before. Most of them could not tell him, including the pastor's wife. A common response was "I don't remember, but I know it was good." His video inspired me to try the same experiment, and I had virtually the same result.

Even if no one ever remembers the words of the preacher, listening to sermons is still important. When we position ourselves under the regular preaching and teaching of God's Word, we open ourselves up to the inspiration of God Himself.

Listen to counsel and accept discipline,
That you may be wise the rest of your days.
Many plans are in a man's heart,
But the counsel of the Lord will stand.
(Proverbs 19:20-21)

Wendy's Story

In my freshman year of college, God called me into Christian Social Ministries. Years later my dad told me he was concerned about that calling because I didn't have "tough enough skin." He was right, but during college God prepared me through two dating relationships that ended in some very traumatic experiences. God used these experiences to develop a tougher skin for me, and He also developed other qualities which would be beneficial in my future counseling work with trauma victims.

As I was working on my Masters of Science in Social Work, I met and married my husband. We had two wonderful children, and I began working for an agency as a daycare consultant, which meant I was providing counseling for traumatized preschoolers at daycare centers throughout the city. One of my first cases involved two little brothers who were in the backseat of their car and saw their mother murdered in the front seat. Another early case was a preschooler whose mother walked in and saw the father sexually abusing the little girl. As a counselor new in the field, heavy cases like these not only needed a tough skin, they required I get quality supervision and guidance from people more experienced than I was.

That job helped prepare me for the next job in which I worked on a team of nine therapists who only dealt with domestic violence families. I led the children's treatment and helped co-lead the treatment groups for the perpetrators and the victim spouses. Again, a therapist doesn't survive being constantly exposed to people in the depths of trauma and abuse if she doesn't find great support and counsel. There were many, many evenings when I would go home, hug my husband and thank him for being a godly man who respected me and was such a great father to our children.

People often asked if I would ever want to be a foster parent, but I always told them I'd never be able to pour myself into the lives of my clients and then come home and have to continue to pour myself out at that same, intense level. God's call on my life was to minister to the hurting through my work. My family life was part of what re-charged my battery and enabled me to continue working with the hurting.

Fast forward. Our second child had left for college, and my husband and I were enjoying the freedom to spend much more time together and go when and where we wanted without taking our children into account. Through a series of circumstances orchestrated by God, we met a young lady who was a refugee. She had an amazing story which involved escaping from slavery and surviving tremendous hardships. Yet despite her history, she was respectful and loving. The three of us began doing things like going to high school football games together, and my husband and I were very happy to have an unofficial third child. God was developing in me an openness toward being a foster parent.

Ultimately, our interactions with this lovely young lady made us receptive to opening our home to a seventeen-year-old young man from Central America. Unfortunately, this wasn't a friendly teenager from a culture that respected their elders; this young man was an angry teenager from a country that was the murder capital of the world.

But God equips us for every challenge, right? God had been equipping me through the past twenty years of work with traumatized children, twelve of those years working with domestic violence. I realized within two weeks of Jaime joining our family I would need every tool God had given me to help God reach Jaime.

In my field of work there is a checklist called ACE: Adverse Childhood Experiences. If you check off as many as three, your odds go up dramatically for all kinds of negative impacts on your life. Jaime's traumatic history checked off eight. Furthermore, Jaime had learned all the emotional, psychological, crazy-making ways of domestic violence perpetrators. As if that wasn't enough, he demonstrated the extremely angry, frustrating, and illogical traits of an attachment disrupted child.

My husband and I did a lot of things right, including believing each other rather than our new son's version of events, going to conferences about how to parent attachment disrupted children, focusing on our marriage relationship so it would remain strong, and going to therapy sessions with our foster son. Despite doing everything we could, and despite the fact that God had been equipping me for years, by the end of six months I knew I couldn't live like this anymore. No one wants to live with a person who is emotionally and mentally abusive, and this little experiment of God's was validating my original idea that I should never be a foster parent. I did not feel like God was telling me I could return Jaime to the foster care system, but I knew our current family situation was failing.

After six months of constant, challenging behaviors and disrupted peace in our home, I was sitting in my rocking chair one Saturday morning. Saturday was usually the day of the week I did not start the day by reading the Bible. This Saturday, however, the thought popped into my head, "God has a message for me," and I immediately went up to my bedroom and sat down with my "Read The Bible Through in a Year" Bible. This is the

132

book I read in my quiet times with God and that day the New Testament reading was from Romans 12. As I read, my attention narrowed to a selection of verses and then honed in on Romans 12: 12: "Be joyful in hope, patient in affliction and faithful in prayer."

I repeatedly read and re-read this verse, wanting to understand the message God had for me. Okay, I thought, what are my hopes for Jaime? This led to filling an 8 ½ x 11 page with my hopes for Jaime, from him being able to understand the value of school in his life to him grasping God's love for him. How can I be patient in this constant affliction? I wrote down all the ways I could think of to feel and demonstrate patience. How can I be faithful in prayer? I wrote down as many ways as I could think of to maintain an attitude of prayer. As I sat and looked at this massive list of hopes for Jaime, I knew the list was too unwieldy for me to take on all at once. So, I grouped hopes that were similar in topic and I ended up with three to four hopes to pray for each day of the week.

Can I tell you life magically changed and all was better? Absolutely not. What I can tell you is when I took my eyes off of the problem and focused on God, my attitude improved, as well as my ability to walk the daily challenges. The saying, "Don't tell God you have a big problem. Tell your problem you have a big God" was proving true. As huge as our problems with Jaime were, God was proving He was bigger.

As I write this, it will soon be six years since God spoke to me through Romans 12:12. I still pray that list of hopes and am excited to let you know God has moved in every single one. Jaime has made more progress than many ever dreamed he could, and he is a fun, integral part of our family fabric. He still has days where he will regress to an old pattern of thinking or behaving, and I try to approach these with the mindset that God continues to use these challenges to not only grow Jaime, but me as well. As it says in the Bible, iron sharpens iron. The most

133

amazing transformation is when we point out Jaime's backsliding to him, he is now willing to take on those old patterns and change them to pro-social ones.

The biggest hope on my list—that Jaime will grasp how much God loves him—has yet to be fully accomplished. Part of me wonders how Jaime can ever grasp the hugeness of God's love when he still doesn't even understand the love I have for him. Then I remember God specifically brought Jaime to our family and "that he who began a good work in you will carry it on to completion until the day of Christ Jesus" (Philippians 1:6).

Author's Note: While Wendy and her husband did everything they could to "sharpen their ax," there are challenges in life that can't be addressed except through absolute dependence on God. While their educational, professional, and personal preparation helped them develop a constructive relationship with Jaime, true success didn't begin until Wendy entrusted Jaime to God in prayer.

Meditation Moment

- Who do you have in your life to whom you can turn to for advice? Who do you have in your life whom you can provide guidance to?

- Are you a lifelong learner? Are you exposing yourself on a regular basis to new ideas through reading and study? Are you part of a support group or a small group that you can turn to for advice and emotional support?

- Are there people you find irritating? What does this irritation tell you about your own heart, and what could God be telling you through your relationships with or exposure to these people?

- Do you seek out and value the advice of your elders? In what ways can you seek out wisdom so one day you will be able to help younger seekers find answers and direction in life?

- Can you think of a time when God used someone or something to "sharpen your ax" in a way which made a difference in your life later? How is God working in you right now, preparing you for changes in your life?

Chapter Eight

Lessons Learned

God sees the gold and silver that will be left behind when we allow Him to teach us, guide us and complete His work which the fire has begun.

There are some mistakes we will never repeat. One of my former supervisors served during Vietnam as commanding officer for an artillery battery. During practice drill, one of his sergeants misread his orders and fired his gun toward town instead of away from it. The fact no one was killed did not make the report to a general the next day any easier. Surprisingly, their meeting was almost over before the general brought up the incident. When he did, the general simply said, "Mister, that is one sergeant who better never make that mistake again! Am I understood?"

Wouldn't it be wonderful if we could learn from mistakes and failures and never do them again? Unfortunately, that is not always the case. Just consider our national divorce rate. According to the online journal Public Discourse of the Witherspoon Institute, approximately 22 percent of adult Americans have been divorced.8 Taking into consideration a fifth of Americans over the age of twenty-five have never been married, that leaves us a long way from the 40-50 percent divorce rate cited by most people. The truth is, people who are divorced once are much more likely to be divorced again. Some even take it to extremes.

I once interviewed a man in his early forties for a position on the church staff. He asked if being divorced was a problem. I told him it depended on the circumstances. He then told me he had been divorced more than once. When I asked how many times, he told me he had been divorced eight times, and his current marriage was his ninth. He reminded me of one of my best friends in college whose father married so many times the son quit attending the weddings after the fifth or sixth ceremony. I had the pleasure of meeting this father. Nice guy—poor marital track record.

When someone fails the same way over and over, it is tempting for them to simply give up and say, "That's just the way I am. I don't do well in ..." The truth is God wants to use our failures to teach us important principles that will help us avoid unnecessary failures as we become more like Jesus.

Our greatest danger zones for repetitive failure are our areas of unrecognized weakness. For many years, one of my weaknesses was in the area of handling conflict and confrontation. As the child of an alcoholic father and a wonderful but enabling mother, there were always issues in our family that needed to be addressed. Unfortunately, no one ever addressed them. Failure was something my family walked around and ignored on a daily basis. It was a skill I learned well.

When I started in the pastorate, despite going to seminary, I honestly did not have a clue what I was doing. Fortunately, there was a retired minister in the church who guided me every step of the way. In truth, he became the de facto pastor and, even though I was called the pastor, I was his associate pastor responsible for outreach and preaching. When my mentor moved away into his retirement home, I had the system down pretty well—Sunday morning, Sunday night, Wednesday night, Tuesday night visitation, summer vacation Bible school. Everything seemed to go pretty well, and the church slowly grew as we went through two building programs.

After I had been with the church for about eight years, Jim, a local missionary, shared with me an excellent book by Bill Easum, Sacred Cows Make Gourmet Burgers: Ministry Anytime, Anywhere, By Anyone. Jim and I met together regularly to discuss the book and, through these discussions, my concept of

137

ministry changed as I saw ways our church could more effectively minister to our community. Attempting to implement these changes led to my first real conflict with church leadership. I decided to put the changes on hold and accepted a full-time missionary position in Utah. I told myself this was to protect the harmony of the church, but I was honestly running away from confrontation and conflict.

Everything in Utah went well until, after about a year and a half, a member of our church's personnel committee asked if I would consider replacing my sponsoring pastor. While I declined, my sponsoring pastor must have somehow found out about the offer because, from that point on, he treated my ministry as a threat. He tried to convince members of our mission church to go to his church instead, and he refused to allow the mission to use its own monies to rent a suitable worship center.

At that time, our mission was meeting in a school whose principal was less than supportive. The principal would not provide air conditioning in the broiling summer or heat in the frigid winter. (Anybody who has lived in Utah knows how extreme both of these seasons can be.) We wore shorts in the summer and parkas in the winter. He also had the school custodian dump trash cans in the middle of our worship area before we arrived.

We desperately wanted a new worship venue, and I found myself deep in conflict with my supervisor without a clue how to handle it. It became apparent to me I had run away from conflict in Jacksonville only to find it in Utah. I decided running was not the answer. It was time to learn, so I passionately studied conflict resolution. After a few weeks, I was ready to address our disagreements directly and constructively.

About this time, my sponsoring pastor and I were scheduled to go on a three-hour drive to a conference. It seemed like a perfect opportunity to let him have an earful of my complaints and concerns. Right before we left, God spoke unmistakably to me through my prayer time. I was to keep my complaints to myself and use the six hours there and back to listen to and learn to love my pastor. For once in my life I was looking forward to confrontation and God told me to shut up.

Looking back, I see a much more important lesson for me to learn than conflict management. There are three biggies in Scripture. Three principles are revealed by two questions that lie at the heart of what the Ministry of Failure is all about.

The first question is found in John 6:28. Jesus was asked, "What shall we do, so that we may work the works of God?" In His answer, Jesus gives us the key to our eternal destiny. He could have responded by saying be good, be baptized, be moral, be sincere in your faith, go to church, or by any of a thousand responses that the Culture of Success allows for. Instead, Jesus answered and said to them, "This is the work of God, that you believe in Him whom He has sent" (John 6:29). The first biggie is faith in Jesus is all we need to fulfill God's law.

The second and third principles came as Jesus answered the question, "Teacher, which is the great commandment in the Law?" In essence, He was being asked, "Teacher, what is the key to a purposeful life?" Jesus said, "You shall love the Lord your God with all your heart, and with all your soul, and with all your mind. This is the great and foremost commandment. The second is like it, you shall love your neighbor as yourself. On these two commandments depend the whole Law and the Prophets" (Matthew 22:27-40).

Principle 1 – Salvation is through faith in Jesus.
Principle 2 – Love the Lord your God with all your heart, and with all your soul, and with all your mind.
Principle 3 – Love your neighbor as yourself.

Life is basic training in applying these three principles. This includes every experience we go through, including our failures. In fact, without love it is impossible to be truly successful in anything. It all becomes failure without love.

> If I speak with the tongues of men and of angels, but do not have love, I have become a noisy gong or a clanging cymbal. If I have the gift of prophecy, and know all mysteries and all knowledge; and if I have all faith, so as to remove mountains, but do not have love, I am nothing. And if I give all my possessions to feed the poor, and if I surrender my body to be burned, but do not have love, it profits me nothing. (I Corinthians 13:1-3)

God intends for us to lovingly approach every aspect of our life. When I was in conflict with my boss, I had no right to confront him until I could do it out of love. The amazing thing was after our long trip together and the work God did in both our hearts, there was no longer any need to confront my pastor. A few weeks later, our mission began meeting in a much nicer location with clean floors, heat, and air conditioning.

The Culture of Success always addresses failure from the viewpoints of process, self-image, and self-improvement. A man facing financial ruin is concerned about how he can improve his bottom line and what people will think of him if he fails. A person facing divorce worries about how to make their marriage stronger and how to explain their marriage failure to others. A student who is failing college worries about how to get his grades up, study more effectively, and whether his or her parents will cut off support. A minister facing church conflict worries about how to minimize the impact on his congregation and how to get through the conflict with his reputation intact.

Failure is more than about process and what others think. It is even more than learning about our weaknesses and how to address them. It is about moving us towards God's ultimate will: glorifying God through our love for Him and for others. Until we follow the Ministry of Failure to that end, we will never learn the lessons God has for us.

In the movie Runaway Bride, there is a great dialogue between Ike Graham, played by Richard Gere, and Ellie Graham, played by Rita Wilson. Their characters are work colleagues who were at one time married. The conversation begins with Ike asking Ellie about the cause of their divorce. When Ellis is elusive, Ike asks if he truly saw her while they were married. When she indicates that he did not, Ike apologizes and Ellie laments that it took twelve years for them to reach this point.

When a person sees who is impacted and how they are impacted by failure—whether spouse, neighbor, children, self, or God—he or she will begin the process of learning the hard lessons of failure. If no one is impacted, that failure fits squarely in the same category as my failed Church Social Ministries class. Other than being something to avoid in the future, it doesn't really matter at all.

Some failures do have greater consequences than others. Consider the failure of pornography, one of the most destructive epidemics the world has ever known. Millions of people in the United States alone are either addicted to or make a regular practice of viewing pornography. The statistics are staggering.

According to a 2016 survey of American men and women by the Barna Group, almost six in ten young adults (57 percent) seek out pornography either daily, weekly, or monthly, and most of these young adults believe failing to recycle is more immoral than pornography. In addition, 37 percent of teens and 29 percent of adults twenty-five years old and older also frequently seek out pornography.

Addiction can be a devastating form of failure. It is a cycle of repetitive failure that makes no allowance for consequences. If you are addicted to pornography, I recommend contacting a biblically based intervention ministry. If you don't have a local option, you may consider one like Pure Life Ministries in Kentucky. They offer a residential program as well as intensive phone counseling. Their website is www.purelifeministries.org.

The American Association of Christian Counselors is another powerful resource in locating professional counselors and residential treatment centers throughout the United States. Their Addiction & Recovery Network resources include quick reference guides which can help anyone who wants to learn more about overcoming addiction and how to help someone who is addicted.

Whether you are addicted to pornography or not, an important step in breaking the cycle of failure is to come to the place where you see everyone involved. See the damage you are doing to your own thought life, spiritual life, and sex life. If you are married, see your spouse and his or her need for the intimacy you are giving to a stranger every time you view pornography. See your spouse's shame, anger, and feelings of inadequacy that come from knowing he or she doesn't satisfy your sexual needs. See your children and the impact you are having on their life. Even if you fantasize your children are not being exposed through your sin, see the spiritual protection you are failing to provide because you are participating in defiant sin. See the people who have been turned into objects of your fantasy for the divinely created people they are.

Covenant Eyes is a useful tool which helps partners maintain a covenant relationship by monitoring each other's computer usage. According to their 2015 Pornography Statistics report, Tanya Burleson, formerly known as Jersey Jaxin, said, "Guys are punching you in the face. You get ripped. Your insides can come out of you. It's never-ending. You're viewed as an object—not as a human with a spirit. People do drugs because they can't deal with the way they're being treated." Is it any wonder many of the most ardent opponents to the sex industry are men and women who once worked in it?

What kind of abuse, degradation, and lack of self-esteem would lead a person to pervert something as beautiful as their own God-given sexuality? Instead of seeing an object of lust, love would see the truth: horrible emotional pain, manipulation, and humiliation.

Lastly, we need to see what viewing porn does to God, Himself. He created men and women. He invented sex for the purpose of marital unity, intimacy, and procreation. Pornography is a slap in God's face which says, "I know better than you do what my needs are, and I am going to satisfy them no matter who I have to use or who I hurt."

Porn, of course, is not the only type of dehumanizing sin. Whatever causes us to choose self-interest above love (lust, greed, pride, rebellion, or any other sin), the first step in truly learning from our failure is to ask God to help us see everyone involved, including ourselves, from God's perspective. The second step is to act accordingly.

It is important we don't wait twelve years (as Ike and Ellie did) to act on what we are learning. Go to the people impacted and be honest. If your failure is moral, confess your sin and ask for forgiveness. Express your concern and love. Discuss with them and focus on their success as much as your own. In other words, love your neighbor as yourself. Accept any accountability and consequences you need to fulfill to make things right for the other parties involved first and yourself second.

According to the Guidelines for Christian Conciliation published by the Institute for Christian Conciliation, the following are fundamental principles we need to follow when seeking reconciliation.

Be honest. (Ephesians 4:25)
Do what is right and merciful. (Micah 6:8)
Accept responsibility for your actions and admit your wrongs. (Matthew 7:5)
Keep your word. (Matthew 5:37)
Be concerned about the interests of others. (Philippians 2:4)
Listen carefully to what others say. (Proverbs 18:13)
Overlook minor offenses. (Proverbs 19:11)
Confront others constructively. (Ephesians 4:29)
Be open to forgiveness and reconciliation. (Ephesians 4:32)
Change harmful attitudes and behavior. (Proverbs 28:13)
Make restitution for any damage you have caused. (Exodus 21:33-34)

As our church went through the reconciliation process, the hardest of these principles for me personally was learning to listen carefully to what others say. I had to learn to keep my mouth shut even when I felt someone was misrepresenting the situation or unfairly attacking me. It is impossible to listen when our mouths are running. It is also hard for someone to feel safe expressing themselves if they know someone is going to interrupt every time they disagree. The reason why learning to love is so hard is because love demands complete sacrificial giving of self. Sometimes this might mean we bite the bullet and actually listen to our enemy. It might mean we make hard decisions like quitting our job so we have more time to spend with our spouse, or resigning from a church position to protect the integrity of a ministry. It might mean giving up a favorite hobby so we have time to talk to our children or accepting accountability or counseling to protect our self and others. Whatever form it takes, it frequently involves giving up our rights so another person can be helped. "We know love by this, that He laid down His life for us; and we ought to lay down our lives for the brethren" (1 John 3:16).

Before and during the business meeting, I was concerned for the process (wanting the church to be healthy). I was concerned about my self-image (wanting people to know each situation had been handled correctly). And I was concerned about self-improvement (making peace in each situation.)

What I did not do was see the men and the church body as a whole being failed by my pride. I saw the men as sources of frustration and aggravation and the church as something to protect. Love for these men and for the body of Christ should have led me months before to kill my pride and involve other leaders in order to use every redemptive resource possible. Love does whatever it takes, within biblical guidelines.

While love is the ultimate lesson learned, the Ministry of Failure teaches us other lessons as well, which prepare us to be more Christ-like. While other people may play a role (or even the primary role) in any failure, when facing such failure, we must take the time to evaluate and learn from our own behaviors, attitudes, and inaction. As Jesus said:

> Why do you look at the speck that is in your brother's eye, but do not notice the log that is in your own eye? Or how can you say to your brother, 'Let me take the speck out of your eye,' and behold, the log is in your own eye? You hypocrite, first take the log out of your own eye, and then you will see clearly to take the speck out of your brother's eye. (Matthew 7:3-5)

We have an amazing capability of ignoring our logs until we find ourselves in a difficult situation that forces us to admit we have a problem. One of the greatest blessings of failure is its ability to bring us to a new level of self-awareness and force us to address areas in our life we would otherwise have been content to ignore. Accepting, confessing, and struggling with our own weaknesses and sinful blind spots makes us less judgmental toward others. It

145

also prepares us to make a positive difference in the lives of others.

Whether we are dealing with prejudice, selfishness, anger, control issues, impatience, covetousness, poor self-control, addiction, laziness, pride, or any other personal failing, we are blessed with the ability to see the situation and the people involved with less distortion after we identify and remove our own logs.

Malachi uses a different illustration of this same process. He refers to God as a "refiner's fire" (Malachi 3:2). A refiner's fire melts down ore, bringing all the junk in the ore (called dross) to the surface where it can be removed. What is left behind is pure gold or silver.

When we mess up and find ourselves in the middle of a fire of our own making, we often hate what we see inside ourselves. This is our dross. It may be the primary cause of our problems and failures or it may be peripheral. It has always been inside of us, yet we are often oblivious to its existence. It is the anger we feel when we fall off the wagon. It is our impatient spirit when we are caught wasting time and money. When we refuse to see this dross by examining our culpability and then seek reconciliation, we short-circuit God's work in our life. The result is usually horribly messy.

Even though God would not allow me to confront my supervisor on our long drive together, the principles I learned during my study of conflict and reconciliation did not go to waste. The next church I went to provided ample opportunities for me to apply the principles learned. After this church's previous pastor left, a man joined who specialized in causing conflict. By the time I arrived, he had spent months starting arguments with younger members of the church, usually over insignificant things. He then intentionally misled the senior adults of the church, telling them he was defending the elderly in the church against the younger members. He claimed the younger members of the church wanted to get rid of all the senior citizens. (I wish I was making this up, but I am not that creative.)

The situation was so tense that when two children who were waiting for their father decided to draw on the chalk board in the empty senior adult room, the first woman who entered the class that morning saw children in her classroom and had a panic attack. She literally ran out of the building screaming, "They are trying to get rid of us!"

My first two days at the church were spent with a parade of people coming to me with stories of conflict, all centered on the same man. While this man agreed to meet with me for counseling, he quickly left the church, leaving many broken relationships behind in the process. He also left with a great deal of anger and frustration. The only other time I ever saw him was in a grocery store when he walked up and threatened to punch me.

While he blamed me for his frustration and loss, I believe his anger came from a hurting heart that refused to honestly examine itself. Whatever form dross takes, seeing it is a wonderful gift from God. It means God is working to help us realize the gold and silver He sees remaining after we allow Him to teach us, guide us, and complete His work which the fire has begun.

Consider it all joy, my brethren, when you encounter various trials, knowing that the testing of your faith produces endurance. And let endurance have its perfect result, so that you may be perfect and complete, lacking in nothing. (James 1:2-4)

Steve Gallagher's Story

My rebellious ways began in sixth grade—throwing eggs at cars, shooting spit wads at teachers, and picking on other kids. By my ninth and tenth grades in high school, I was using drugs and getting high virtually every day. Barbiturates, methamphetamines, opium, heroin, marijuana, LSD, mescaline, and peyote would all eventually become a regular part of my life.

When I was fifteen, two significant events occurred in my life. I went to my first Hell's Angel's party, and I had sex with my first girl. Eventually, I was expelled from school and attended a school for troubled teens where I openly smoked pot in school and planted marijuana seeds in the teacher's flowerbox. To get money, I began dealing drugs and burglarizing homes.

By the time I was twenty-five, I had overcome my drug addiction, spent some time in the Jesus Movement as a Jesus Freak, become addicted to sex, and been married and divorced.

In January of 1979, I renewed an acquaintance with an old friend named Gale. One day I walked into the shack Gale called home, and two things stood out in great contrast: the place was incredibly filthy, but like a rose blooming in the middle of a dung heap, there stood a pretty little blond warming her back on the wall heater. I was immediately drawn to Kathy when I met her—so much so I began hanging around their house in the hopes of running into her. Although I struck up conversations with her every chance I got, she remained aloof. She was estranged from her husband and, after what she had been through with him, she had no interest in becoming involved with another man. However, to my surprise and delight, Gale and his wife seemed anxious to match-make us.

With their encouragement, and my insistence, Kathy finally agreed to go on a date with me. I continued to pursue her, but she kept her distance. Finally, in a bold move, I asked her to spend a weekend with me at a beachside resort in Santa Cruz. Afterward, we moved in together and got married.

148

Our marriage had major ups and downs from the very start. While Kathy eventually became a Christian and was trying to make our marriage work, she had long since given up attempting to serve God. I am sure my addiction to sex had something to do with this since I had once again begun to frequent adult bookstores and massage parlors.

The fiery love Kathy once had for the Lord had now become an ember which was about to be completely extinguished. She was being pulled in two different directions: serve God or please her husband. My indifference to our marriage only compelled her to seek my approval all the more. Gradually, she slid away from God until she finally gave up all pretenses of being a Christian.

One night I mentioned to her that John Holmes was in the jail where I worked. She asked me who he was, and I explained he was a famous porn star. I used this conversation to introduce my wife to X-rated movies. As we watched them together, the illicit culture expressed in the videos altered our perspectives of marriage, lovemaking, and even life itself. What was once a natural expression of physical intimacy—only one aspect of many that make up a marriage—was now magnified into the centerpiece of our relationship. I looked forward to the weekends when a pornographic video would serve as the highlight to our own private sex party.

This mutual mindset emboldened me to tell her about my visits to prostitutes and massage parlors. I was so oblivious to her feelings that I never considered how this would affect her. It relieved me to be honest with her, and I convinced myself I was doing the right thing. The truth was that it crushed her emotionally.

At first, I was very excited when Kathy and I watched movies together. I had actually started treating her with kindness. However, it wasn't long before I became dissatisfied again. As that happened, my anger surfaced. I constantly berated and verbally abused her. I was so utterly self-absorbed I had no comprehension whatsoever for how I had beaten her down as a person. Unbeknownst to me, she had finally reached her limit.

One night I got home sometime after 2:00 a.m. My heart sank as I opened the door to the apartment. Lying on the floor in front of the door was a note from my wife. I grabbed the scrap of paper and read it. She said she was sorry to hurt me like this but just couldn't take anymore. I was shocked because (in my delusion) I had imagined our relationship was fine. Now, all I could think of was how stupid I had been to treat her like I had.

I was very upset, yet knew there was nothing I could do to bring her back. Although there was a side to me that wanted the freedom which comes with bachelorhood, I still loved her. I felt so crushed I sought solace through other women. Within a few days I had initiated relationships with two different women. I missed my wife, but made up my mind I would make the best of the situation.

About a week after Kathy left, I met a woman at a party. For the next couple of weeks, we became inseparable. I began staying at her place more than my own. Kathy was becoming a distant memory to me.

One Saturday morning, I awoke at this woman's apartment with an inexplicable longing to get Kathy back. It seemed so strange to have this feeling, because I had become content with my new single lifestyle. I called my mother in Sacramento and asked her what I should do. She told me my only hope was to turn my life over to God and to start praying and fasting.

I said, "I might consider living as a Christian if Kathy comes back to me, but there's no way I can do it without her."

"It will never work that way, Steve," she replied.

Her words kept going through my mind that evening at work. The next morning, I called Shirley, my mother-in-law. She told me Kathy had been gone a few days with a friend. She went on to tell me the Lord had revealed to her it was His will for our marriage to be restored. Kathy's sister, Linda, had experienced the same sense. Considering how angry they had been with me, it was obvious to me God was at work. She had more to say, though. "Steve, I gotta tell you, Kathy is dead-set against ever coming back to you. In fact, she has filed for divorce." Little did I know the friend she was with was some guy she had met.

Ten minutes after I got to work on Monday, I was told I had a phone call. My heart raced as I went into the busy office to answer it. It was Kathy. She asked me a couple of questions about our taxes but was very cold and distant. She said she hadn't talked to her mom lately, and I suggested she should. She made it clear she was only calling for business purposes.

I was miserable that whole evening at work. Because I was stationed at the front desk, I didn't get back to eat my supper in the deputy "chow hall" until late. The only deputy still there was a Christian guy named Willie. He could see I was upset.

"What's wrong, Gallagher?"

I explained the whole situation to him. As we talked, sex with other women suddenly seemed so unimportant to me. "Willie, I don't know what to do," I finally lamented.

"Why don't you ask the Lord to forgive you of your sins and put this whole mess into His hands?" he suggested.

I agreed and bowed my head right there at the table. "Lord, I know I have been sinful and have rebelled against you. I repent of my sin and ask you to take control of my life once again. Please forgive me of my sins and straighten out my life."

It was the first time I had ever really given Him everything. Instantly, I was filled with peace of mind.

The next day, I tried to explain it to my girlfriend, but she couldn't understand. "What does God have to do with us?" she wanted to know. Even though she couldn't understand my reasons, I knew I had to break up with her. This deepened my sense of peace. That night after work, I became very troubled. The only thing I could think about was how I could get Kathy back. All night long I tossed and turned as I cried out to God to send my wife back to me. Sometime during the night, I received my answer from Him. It was almost a voice I could hear, yet it didn't come into my mind through my ears. All I heard was, "She will call you tomorrow."

I didn't sleep much and finally forced myself to get up. I decided to drive down the street to a fast-food restaurant. Wait a minute, I can't do that, I thought to myself, Kathy's going to call. Just as soon as I thought that, the realization came to me that if she was going to call it would be God's doing. He would have her call when I was there. I went to eat and returned in about half an hour. She called ten minutes later.

As soon as she identified herself, I began pouring my heart out to her. I told her I had turned my life over to the Lord and that I wanted her back. "I prayed all night last night, and you may not believe this, but God told me you were going to call!" I exclaimed. She was listening but was very noncommittal. "Have you talked to your mom since we talked the other day?" I asked. "No," she replied.

"Well, why don't you call her up and give me a call back." I had no idea the kind of battle going on inside her. Kathy had absolutely no intention of coming back to me. She had found a man who treated her like a princess and believed she would be a fool to return. Then she called her parents.

152

The telephone rang a few minutes later. "My parents said God told them we should get back together," she told me. "But there's just one problem. I have a boyfriend. Do you want me to come over so we can talk?"

"Yes," I instantly replied.

She arrived a few minutes later and explained what had happened. I was just happy to have her back. We spent the night together. It seemed like old times, although she was very upset because she felt so much guilt about having committed adultery. The next morning, she called Tim and told him she was staying with me. She started crying because now she felt guilty about hurting him. He told her he was packing and going to San Diego to be with his family. She had to go to the house they had been living in to get her stuff, but we decided she should wait until later, when he was sure to be gone.

About 12:30, she called the house to make sure Tim wasn't there. Nobody answered, so she left to go over there. As she was getting ready to go, she said, "Steve, pray I'll have the strength to leave him."

"What do you mean by that?" I questioned.

"Nothing," she said as she walked out the door.

She had been gone for about an hour when I got on my knees by my bed and began thanking God for everything, especially for bringing us back together. I prayed He would give her strength, if she needed it for some reason, to leave that house. Tears were soon streaming down my cheeks as I realized how much God had done for me. I begged Him to send her back to me. "Why did You put us back together, just to turn around and allow us to split up again?" I demanded to know. After I prayed for another half an hour, the phone rang. I answered it, but it was only a dial tone. At that point, a foreboding feeling swept over me. Suddenly, I realized I could not survive the night without her. I knew I would commit suicide if she didn't come back to me. I began shaking out of fear because I knew my life was about to end. I was literally in fear for my life.

Just then, I remembered a crumpled piece of paper which was in my pocket. It was the phone number of a pastor I had met at the jail. Not knowing what else to do, I called him up and quickly gave him a rundown of the situation. He told me he didn't have a car right then but would try to get one. As we talked, the operator suddenly cut in on the conversation. "I have an emergency phone call from Kathy. Will you clear the line?" she asked.

"Yes!" I blurted out.

"Praise the Lord, brother. That's God working," the preacher said.

I hung up the phone, waiting for her to call. Seconds ticked by and it didn't ring. Several minutes came and went. Still no phone call. I became overwhelmed with a dark despair. I was so filled with internal anguish, I literally writhed on the floor crying out to God to bring her back. Jesus described hell as being a place where there will be weeping and gnashing of teeth. This perfectly describes the deep agony of soul I was experiencing. I was clenching my teeth so tightly it seemed as though I would break my jaw. I lay on the floor grasping the carpet with such intensity my knuckles were white. Nothing was going to relieve that agony except for her return.

I had been upset and depressed when Kathy had left me, but what I experienced that day was an internal torment which could not be explained by the loss of a loved one. It was something much deeper. I called the pastor again and told him she hadn't called back. He said he would come over as soon as he could get a car. I didn't know if Tim was holding her against her will or if she had

154

just decided she didn't want to come back to me. "Why, oh why, did I let her leave by herself?" I despaired.

It was about 3:30 when the pastor showed up at the front door; three hours since Kathy had left. Seeing him helped a little. He was only there about two minutes when the phone rang. As soon as the pastor arrived, Kathy got through. "Hello!" I answered with great urgency.

"It's me." The cold tone had returned to her voice.

"Where are you? What are you doing?" I wanted to know.

"Steve, I love Tim, and I'm not coming back to you."

"You don't love him, you love me! I'm your husband!" I exclaimed.

"Steve, I can't come back."

When she said that, I grabbed my off-duty revolver which was sitting on the coffee table and twirled the cylinder by the mouthpiece of the phone. It made a loud click as I slammed the cylinder into place. "You hear that? You can just sit there and listen to me blow my brains out!" With that I put the gun to my head.

The chaplain began frantically jumping up and down yelling, "Lady, he means it! He's gonna' do it!"

Just then, Kathy screamed into the phone, "Steve, don't do it!"

When she did that, her boyfriend Tim grabbed her arm, and she looked up at him. He looked completely different. Evil permeated his face. It was as if the angel of light was suddenly revealed for who he really was.

155

"Kathy," he sneered at her, "if he wants to kill himself, let him do it. It's not your fault!"

Then she realized this man was no prince. He was demon possessed.

When she said that, I pulled the gun away from my head.

Now, she understood she was in the wrong place but was too frightened to leave. She also was still very confused. The preacher got on the phone and prayed with her. He ordered the spirits of confusion to leave her alone and pleaded for God's intervention. Instantly, she knew what she should do. It was a violent struggle of life and death in the spiritual world. I just kept praying.

Kathy agreed to meet me at the pastor's church. As I waited for her, it seemed like forever. She finally called and said she was lost. I raced over to where she was. All I could do was hold her in my arms. It was 6:30 and had been the longest six hours of my life.

It was hard for me to understand why these six hours had been so devastating. It had only been a couple of days before I was experiencing the thrill of a new relationship. Everything was going fine. I still missed Kathy, but I was well on my way to getting over her. Why did I suddenly feel such a need for her? And then, when she did show up and leave again, why did I become so completely overwhelmed by despair that I was ready to kill myself?

After my mind cleared, I was able to look at the situation more objectively. It was God who was at work in that situation. He allowed me to really see Kathy, myself, and my failure in our marriage for the first time. He had put the sense in me that I could not live without her. In myself, I had already given up on her, and she had given up on me. That was why there was no hope for our marriage, because neither one of us cared enough any longer to fight for it. However, God had different plans. He could see what the future held if we remained together. He also knew it would take something drastic before I would really commit myself to Him and to her.

This battle had left me in emotional shambles and deeply shaken. I had always been so independent and self-reliant, priding myself on the fact I didn't need anyone. Now, suddenly, I knew I had to follow God.

Author's Note: Steve Gallagher is the Founder and Chairman of the Board for Pure Life Ministries and the author of numerous books including Irresistible to God and At the Altar of Sexual Idolatry. This testimony is just a glimpse into his most recent book, Out of the Depths of Sexual Sins: The Story of My Life and Ministry, in which he shares more of his amazing journey.

Steve's turning point was when he saw his sin and his wife's value. Had he not done so, Steve would probably be a divorced prison guard, working on his third marriage, and the thousands of people powerfully touched by Steve's ministry may still be mired in the pain of sexual addiction.

Meditation Moment

- A poem written in the 1800s describes a man whom everyone admires. He is the epitome of a fine gentleman until he goes home and blows his brains out.9 It is impossible to see what is inside another person. While our knowledge is limited, our love does not have to be. We can see people with the eyes of God. How do you want God to see you?

- Process, self-improvement, and self-image are not in themselves bad things. They are, however, incomplete. What failures in your life could have been avoided or transformed had you been motivated by love?

- There are certain people the Bible tells us to avoid. Titus 3:10-11 tells us to reject divisive, angry men who will not respond to godly counsel. 2 Timothy 3:7-9 tells us to reject false teachers in the church who oppose godly leadership. How can rejecting someone be an act of love? What are the dangers in applying this principle?

- When Jesus tells us to love our enemies, He is calling us to extend the Kingdom of God into a failed relationship. How can you express love to an enemy, and what impact could this have on your relationship with that person? There is always the danger you might open yourself up and yet fail to get them to listen or even acknowledge your attempt. Are you willing to take that risk? What steps can you take to get around a wounded heart?

- Has God recently revealed any logs in your life you need to remove in order to be more effective in helping other people?

Chapter Nine

The Church

Our Father thinks we are much, much more than the sum of our failures.

As a student, I went through a lot of jobs, sometimes working two and three part-time jobs at a time. Some were extremely difficult, and some were dream jobs for a student. My favorite was being the night watchman at a business where I was expected to verify every door was locked and then sleep until the morning watchman arrived. They even provided me with a bed. My second favorite job was providing company for a ninety-five-year-old man whose nurse left as I arrived. He didn't require any special care, just someone to talk to until he went to bed. While he slept, I was allowed to study, sleep, or watch television.

What made the second job especially enjoyable was my employer's stories. He loved to talk about his career in professional baseball. He played early in the history of the game when most professional players were paid from game to game. He and a friend traveled around the country having adventures while playing baseball for various teams. One of his favorite stories was about discovering a beached whale which they quickly claimed, slaughtered, and profited from by selling its oil and blubber.

Profit was probably his favorite topic. He made a fortune buying and selling land for the oil industry and was extremely proud of his son who was a wealthy owner of two successful magazines. One evening he showed me a well-worn book titled, He Who Dies with The Most Toys Wins. I knew the man was very materialistic, but he still surprised me when he declared the book was his bible. He said he firmly believed the purpose of life was to accumulate the most material wealth possible.

While few people consciously make a religion out of financial success, the Culture of Success does measure personal value based on how we compare one to another. "What was his net worth when he died?" is a common question for a celebrity or a wealthy individual. A billionaire once declared in an interview that, after a certain point, personal wealth was just a matter of keeping score. I cannot remember whether the cut-off point he mentioned was $30,000,000 or $300,000,000, but either one begs the question, "How much is enough?"

Whether we keep score by wealth, education, or employment status, in the Culture of Success there is always someone with whom to compare yourself. I was a poor student who was given a free trip by our government to spend the summer with my parents in Liberia, Africa. Back home, I was living day to day off my part-time jobs and drove a sad 1964 Oldsmobile borrowed from my aunt. Every day, I automatically poured a quart of oil into this car to keep it going.

As I was walking along a beach in Liberia thinking about how different things were there, a young man ran up to me shouting,

"You American. You rich! You rich!"

I tried to say I wasn't rich, but he cut me off.

"Do you have a car?" he asked.

I said "Yes" and intended to qualify it by describing my borrowed jalopy but he cut me off again.

"Then you are rich!"

Perhaps the culture in Liberia wasn't as different from the American Culture of Success as I had thought. We all seem to compare ourselves with ourselves and make qualitative decisions on who lives up to our standards and who does not. We tend to accept those who live up to our standards, be awed by those who surpass our standards, and disdain those who fall short. While this is natural in our Culture of Success, it is not new. The apostle Paul had to chastise the Corinthian church for this tendency. "You are looking at things as they are outwardly" (II Corinthians 10:7). Paul goes on to admit (vs. 10) that he fell short of the Corinthian standards. "For they say, 'His letters are weighty and strong, but his personal presence is unimpressive and his speech contemptible.'"

Paul did not reject their criticism. Instead, he embraced it. "Now I, Paul, myself urge you by the meekness and gentleness of Christ—I who am meek when face to face with you, but bold toward you when absent" (II Corinthians 10:1).

Today, we would say Paul did not dress for success. He wrote well but had a weak personal presentation. Paul did not push himself on anyone and failed to assert his authority unless he had to. While this led some in the Corinthian church to disdain Paul, Paul counters by saying:

> For we dare not class ourselves or compare ourselves with those who commend themselves. But they, measuring themselves by themselves, and comparing themselves among themselves, are not wise. (II Corinthians 10:12 NKJV)

Jesus also proves how foolish it is to assign value to people through self-comparison. He did not live up to any expectations the world had for Him. He was a poor man from a poor family. He never had a formal education. He wasn't even a good-looking man. Isaiah 53:2 says "He has no stately form or majesty that we should look upon Him, nor appearance that we should be attracted to Him." Jesus would have been a very poor choice for the role of James Bond or any other successful leading man.

I believe one of the reasons Pilate placed the charge of The King of the Jews above Jesus' head when He was crucified was to mock the men who had demanded Jesus' crucifixion. Their argument that Jesus had to be crucified because he claimed to a king was ludicrous. Nobody in their right mind could believe this unattractive, poor, humble, uneducated carpenter, whose followers fled at the first sign of trouble, could compete with Caesar. His background and appearance just didn't fit into the Culture of Success.

In addition, only two of the apostles even came close to fitting into the Culture of Success. Matthew was a tax collector, but he left it all behind to follow Jesus. The only other disciple who showed financial and political savvy was Judas. Some people believe Judas' betrayal of Jesus was not because Judas didn't believe in Jesus but because Judas was tired of Jesus' poverty and wanted to force Him to set up His earthly Kingdom. According to this theory, Judas' betrayal stemmed from his desire to rule. I do not know what motivated Judas, but I do know none of the disciples before or after the resurrection ever experienced the worldly success Judas apparently longed for. As Jesus said to Pilate, "My kingdom is not of this world" (John 18:36).

"Why did You allow that to happen, God?" is sometimes the heart cry of a person who is experiencing the pain of a world which does not ultimately satisfy. An advertising campaign for Dos Equis beer has featured "The Most Interesting Man in the World" since 2006. The role was originally played by Jonathan Goldsmith. When Goldsmith retired from the role, Dos Equis sent him off to Mars on a one-way trip declaring, "His only regret is not knowing what regret feels like." If we all lived life without regret, who would feel a need for more? If this life were perfect, why would we seek the Kingdom of God?

The fact that Jesus did not even try to live up to the expectations of the Culture of Success is a powerful indictment of the way we look at ourselves and others. Rather than compare ourselves with ourselves, we might want to consider how we compare to Jesus Christ. If we choose that standard, we fail miserably. A famous essay titled One Solitary Life ends with a surprising conclusion:

> Nineteen long centuries have come and gone, and today He is a centerpiece of the human race and leader of the column of progress. I am far within the mark when I say that all the armies that ever marched, all the navies that were ever built, all the parliaments that ever sat, and all the kings that ever reigned, put together, have not affected the life of man upon this earth as powerfully as has that one solitary life.[10]

How could one Man who was such a failure by the world's standards make such a difference? Perhaps it is because people throughout the centuries have discovered what even the enemies of Jesus knew: "The Son of Man came eating and drinking, and they say, 'behold, a gluttonous man and a drunkard, a friend of tax collectors and sinners!'" (Matthew 11:19).

If it is foolish to find your value comparing yourself to others, it is wise to find your value in the friendship of Jesus Christ. This truth is the basis of one of my favorite songs, "Someone Worth Dying For," by a group called Mike's Chair. The cross is proof that God sees in each of us someone important enough for divine sacrifice.

It is in our failure and the grace of the Cross that we discover how much He loves us. If we were all Jonathan Goldsmith and lived a regret-free life, we might deceive ourselves into believing God loves us because we deserve to be loved. The fact that we have regrets and know how badly we fail to live up to the Culture of Success is one of the greatest gifts the Ministry of Failure can give us. If God thinks I am worth dying for with all my faults, then He must really love me. And if God can love me like that, what right do I have to think any less of anybody else?

A side effect of this love is that cultural distinctions of pride are absolutely meaningless. This is why, from the very beginning of Christianity, the church has been the one place in society where the distinctions of wealth and status are not to be accepted.

Early in my Christian life, I was deeply proud of my church. It was the fastest growing church in the state of Texas for several years in a row. You can imagine how disappointed I was one Sunday when we had a special visitor. The manager of an extremely successful and famous NFL running back attended the church. He told our pastor he believed he would be able to convince this running back to speak at the church. Since the athlete was a household name and could be a strong draw for visitors, our pastor thought it was a great idea and arrangements were made.

Before the football player spoke, he met with our pastor, who was shocked to learn the running back wasn't a Christian. Since the service was to occur in a few minutes, and it had been heavily advertised, they agreed the athlete would limit his talk to drug abuse and the NFL.

When the running back entered the worship service, he strutted with the confidence of a young man who was used to the adulation of millions—and he wasn't disappointed. Virtually the entire congregation gave him a standing ovation. Even though I was a brand-new Christian and far, far from spiritual, giving a man a standing ovation during a worship service because of his football fame didn't seem right. There are only two people I believe the church should stand up for. One is Jesus Christ. The second is someone who comes to Jesus and finds their salvation.

My brethren, do not hold your faith in our glorious Lord Jesus Christ with an attitude of personal favoritism. For if a man comes into your assembly with a gold ring and dressed in fine clothes, and there also comes in a poor man in dirty clothes, and you pay special attention to the one who is wearing the fine clothes, and say, "You sit here in a good place," and you say to the poor man, "You stand over there, or sit down by my footstool," have you not made distinctions among yourselves, and become judges with evil motives?

If, however, you are fulfilling the royal law according to the Scripture, "You shall love your neighbor as yourself," you are doing well. But if you show partiality, you are committing sin and are convicted by the law as transgressors. (James 2:1-4, 8, 9)

If you are a follower of Jesus Christ, the three most important formative relationships in your life are your relationship with God, your family, and your church. Church is the spiritual family for failures. Paul was speaking of the church when he said:

For consider your calling, brethren, that there were not many wise according to the flesh, not many mighty, not many noble; but God has chosen the foolish things of the world to shame the wise, and God has chosen the weak things of the world to shame the things which are strong ... so that no man may boast before God. But by His doing you are in Christ Jesus, who became to us wisdom from God, and righteousness and sanctification, and redemption, so that, just as it is written, "Let him who boasts, boast in the Lord." (I Corinthians 1:26-31)

165

That is the calling of the church, to be the family of the foolish, the weak, and the common so we can join our hearts together in worship and "boast in the Lord."

One of my many part-time jobs was as a food warehouse inventory clerk at Bassham Foods in Austin, Texas. I worked the night crew, which was probably one of the most unusual warehouse crews in the country. It was almost entirely made up of college and seminary students. My co-workers included the son of an African chieftain and several men working on their doctorates.

Of all the men I worked with, one has a special place in my memory. He was a little rougher than the other dock workers. He had more tattoos, and his language was a little more laced with colorful words. I had the privilege of learning about his life journey as I worked off and on with him for several years. He had been a member of a biker gang, which was not the kind of gang made up of accountants and lawyers on weekends. It was a gang you don't want stopping in your town at night.

As a member of the gang, he fell in love with and married one of the women who traveled with them. Unfortunately, their marriage failed, and they decided to get a legal divorce. On their way to a lawyer's office, they drove by a church where he stopped his motorcycle and asked his wife if she would be willing to try church. It was, after all, something they had never done before and might make a difference. She agreed and, since they could hear people singing, they went inside.

When visitors come to a church, especially a small or medium-size church, it can either be a cause for joy or a cause for concern. If the visitors are obviously people with deep needs, it is tempting for a church that is steeped in the Culture of Success to ignore the visitors or even actively discourage their attendance. After all, it is hard enough to keep everyone in the church happy without bringing in new problems. People leave churches all the time, sometimes expressing the smallest, most insignificant reasons for leaving. When a church is focused on keeping its own members comfortable, the visit of a new, high-needs couple can be overwhelming.

I praise God my biker friend and his wife attended a church that understood the Ministry of Failure. Not only were they warmly greeted, they heard the gospel of Jesus Christ for the first time. After the service, they both bowed in prayer and surrendered their heart to follow Jesus Christ. I met him a few short years later when, still married to the same woman, he had a deep joy from serving Jesus with his whole heart.

This is the Ministry of Failure and the calling of the Church.

The church that welcomed the NFL player was a very rich church. By that I mean there were numerous millionaires who attended regularly. Nobody flouted their wealth, but it was evident in many ways. One Sunday evening, for example, with only a small portion of the church attending, a special collection resulted in enough money to pay off the church operating budget for months. At the same time, there was one man who didn't seem to fit in with the rest of the church. He came every day in his service as the janitor. I watched him faithfully work week after week. and I seldom saw anyone talk to him. I was so impressed by the man's dedication that I went out of my way to get to know him. He was an older, humble, dedicated believer in Jesus Christ who hoped his service made the church a better place for people to experience God.

During one of our conversations he told me while he worked two jobs and his wife worked three in order to make ends meet, things were going to change soon. I asked him what he meant, and he told me his wife had an aunt who was terminally ill. As her aunt's only remaining relative, his wife was going to inherit a fortune. I asked him how much that would be and he said he did not know, but part of it was in a trust fund supporting a local hospital. He estimated it at tens of millions.

The cynic and the hypocrite in me wonders if the ministry of my church to that janitor would have changed at all if they had known he was soon to be a multi-millionaire.

I describe myself as a hypocrite because in all my years of preaching, the only "blessed poor" I have ever preached about have been the "poor in spirit." There is something uncomfortable about God blessing people in financial failure, yet allowing them to remain in poverty. "Listen, my beloved brethren: did not God choose the poor of this world to be rich in faith and heirs of the kingdom?" (James 2:5).

While it might make us uncomfortable, there are many examples in the Bible of people who were financial failures and who were also blessed eternally. Paul, for example, describes the apostles of Jesus Christ:

> We are both hungry and thirsty, and are poorly clothed, and are roughly treated, and are homeless; and we toil, working with our own hands; when we are reviled, we bless; when we are persecuted, we endure; when we are slandered, we try to conciliate; we have become as the scum of the world, the dregs of all things, even until now (I Corinthians 4:11-13).

The Faith Hall of Fame in Hebrews 11 refers to godly people who "went about in sheepskins, in goatskins, being destitute, afflicted, ill-treated (men of whom the world was not worthy), wandering in deserts and mountains and caves and holes in the ground." You don't get much poorer than that. While these people lived completely outside the Culture of Success, God declared they "gained approval through their faith" (Hebrews 11:37, 38).

168

In Luke 16, Jesus told a parable which involved two men: a poor man named Lazarus and a very successful rich man Jesus did not name. Jesus said Lazarus was homeless, sleeping at the rich man's gate and was covered with sores. The only compassion Lazarus knew came from the local dogs who came up and licked his sores. When the two men eventually died, Lazarus was carried up to paradise while the rich man entered torment.

Your financial success or failure does not make you more spiritual. Poverty also does not disqualify us from spiritual greatness. I have known several people over the years who have knowingly risked or sacrificed their financial success in order to do the right thing and pursue God's calling. One of the godliest families I ever met was a foster family in Jacksonville. The father of the family had been a successful banker when he felt the calling to leave it behind and devote himself to raising special needs children. While it was a disastrous decision financially, I have never known a family so blessed by God with unconditional love.

While we must always fight poverty, we will never overcome it. Even if God gave us the resources to end financial poverty, there is a poverty of the spirit that can be even more debilitating and which is not limited to the destitute. Financially, the people of faith described in the above passages were as poor as people in the poorest slum in the world. But their hope, security, and joy were not diminished by their circumstances, because they understood what it meant to be part of the family of God and to gain approval through their faith. God was with them, and their walk with Him gave them hope and peace.

Sam Adeyemi is a well-known author, speaker, and pastor from Nigeria. When he started his church, his ministry was reaching needy people who were far different from the successful people he believed were required to impact Nigeria for Jesus. People were coming to worship asking for bus money to pay for the ride home. Every time he turned around, someone was asking for help with food or bills. At the same time, he was a poor church planter and had nothing to offer them.

As he prayed about it, God told him the members he wanted were the members he had. It was his job as a needy pastor to help his needy members discover their spiritual identity and discover how to begin living as God's children.

Pastor Adeyemi had to learn to look beyond the Culture of Success and see the spiritual potential, identity, and inheritance of every believer. (Rick Warren once described this inheritance as "the riches ... of his grace ... kindness ... patience ... glory ... wisdom ... power ... and mercy.")11 Pastor Adeyemi then had to structure his church so every person had an opportunity to learn and apply the life-changing truths of the Bible—not so their circumstances would change, but so they could experience the power and joy of living out their relationship with God in their circumstances.

In Luke 15, we find the story of a father who had two sons. One of the sons demanded his inheritance early, went away, and wasted it. Eventually, he ruined his life to the point where he found himself slopping hogs and wishing he could eat so well. It was about as low as a Jew could go. The other son stayed home and dutifully served his father.

While living far from his father, the wasteful son experienced the depth of his sin through the Ministry of Failure. The resulting change in his perspective gave him a humble clarity, which was never part of his life agenda. He saw his failure. He saw his need. He saw the honor of being a servant in his father's house.

When this repentant son returned to his father, he found to his relief his father was not turned off by his stench. His father did not scream at him for wasting his fortune. His father was not even interested in any speeches. Instead, his father ran to meet him, embraced him in a bear hug of love. The father then

170

restored his son's honor by giving him symbols of their relationship: sandals, robe, and a ring. As if that wasn't enough, the father made sure no one could miss his extravagant love for his son by returning his son to the bosom of family and community through a wonderful feast (Luke 15:22-24).

While this failure is well known, we often forget the good son also failed. He failed to celebrate his brother's homecoming and was chastised by his father for doing so. At the same time, the good son was promised the grace of his inheritance despite his selfish, shortsighted, jealous attitude. The only true hero in this story is the father whose love covered both son's failures.

There are many different types of churches with many different forms of ministry. But more important than the form is the spirit and purpose of ministry. True worship is a gathering of grateful sons and daughters to experience their Father and encourage each other. Whenever the Church humbly and lovingly gathers together, the Ministry of Failure makes us thrilled to be simple servants in the house of our Father and rejoice in our Father's extravagant embrace of grace, love, and forgiveness. It is within this embrace of worship and truth that we taste the reality of our salvation and eternal inheritance. If you are a believer, this is your feast of joy and where God and His family celebrate together. We celebrate because of Who our Father is and because our Father thinks we are much, much more than the sum of our failures. We are someone worth dying for.

If you are not a believer and have never experienced the embrace of the Father, there is one sure way to earn a standing ovation. "I tell you, there is joy in the presence of the angels of God over one sinner who repents" (Luke 15:10). The angels themselves celebrate when someone humbly enters the Kingdom of God.

Allen and Bob's Story

Carl: Allen, can you tell me what Adopt-A-Block is?

Allen: Adopt-A-Block is an effort by Christians to touch a specific area of need with help and hope in order to let people see Jesus in us and through building relationships, show people the love of God, encouraging them to form or deepen their own relationship with Him.

Carl: And how long have you gentlemen been involved in Adopt-A-Block?

Bob: Here in York, almost five years. I did two years prior in two different trailer parks.

Allen: I am working on my fifth year.

Carl: Something happened recently to you, Allen, in Adopt-A-Block. Can you share what happened?

Allen: On November 16th we were here at the house celebrating Thanksgiving dinner with children and some of the women in the neighborhood, and about halfway through that event there was a knock on the door. I went to the door. There was a kid there looking for another kid. I told him the person he was looking for wasn't here. A guy passing by said something about leaving those kids alone. I did not realize he was on some kind of drugs such as PCP or something similar. This man stepped up on the porch. I thought he was going to say something to me. Instead he blindsided me with a punch that knocked me out. I came back to consciousness when he kicked me in the chest so hard it snapped me out of unconsciousness. I was conscious long enough to grab his leg. I don't know what I thought I could do, but he continued to pound me and slam my head into the wall of the porch. Then my little hero, a hundred-and-five-pound Hispanic grandmother, sixty-five years old, jumped on his back when he wasn't looking and stuck her two-inch acrylic nails into his eyes. He let go. I am convinced that saved my life.

Carl: How bad were your injuries?

Allen: Thank God, I did not have any head injuries. It really messed up my chest and shoulder area. I couldn't lie down and sleep on my back for almost six weeks. For the first week I slept in a chair, but that wasn't going to work because my legs weren't getting any relief and they started to swell, so I got a wedge pillow I could sleep on. But I had a lot of pain for two of three weeks. My face cleared up quicker than I thought it would. I still have a twinge every now and then in my shoulder. It has basically cleared up, however.

Carl: How is this woman who jumped on the man attacking you related to you?

Allen: She is just a lady on the block. A lady we minister to. We have been in her house many times. She has had some addiction problems. Her children have had some addiction problems. They have been in and out of jail, but we are trying to minister to the block, and she was part of that ministry. She was here for a Bible study and dinner with her little daughter. When she heard me fall and other noises, she came to investigate. That was when she saw him attacking me and jumped on his back. God used her, I believe, to save my life.

Carl: It is amazing that she would intervene like that. Does it surprise you?

Allen: Well, I asked her about that. I asked her if she was afraid, and she said she didn't think about it. She said she just saw he was hurting me (she called me her pastor), and she didn't even think. She just jumped on him and did anything she could to stop it.

Carl: Did you have second thoughts about continuing with Adopt-A-Block after that?

Allen: Oh, that had nothing to do with it. First off, he didn't belong on this block. He was from somewhere near Dover. He wasn't even from around here. Just happened to be on the block. Just happened to be high. The people on the block had nothing to do with it. As a matter of fact, when I came back to the block, the whole block knew about it, and I had adult men coming to me (Hispanic men who are not quick to show their feelings) with tears in their eyes, expressing their thanks that I was doing better and that they were glad to see me. I didn't think about it. I really don't think about it now. It has probably made me more cautious, being aware of what is going on around me, but it doesn't keep me from going out. I don't worry about it.

Carl: The relationships you have described is one of the things that has amazed me about Adopt-A-Block. From the very first time I went out with Adopt-A-Block, I was amazed by your relationship with people who live on the block, Bob, and I was wondering if you could share about the type of relationship you have with the people.

Bob: One of the first times we were visiting the blocks, there were only about five or six of us doing it. At that time, we met at a corner restaurant and would go out from there. As we went out, I noticed some teenagers at the top of a hill, and it was clear it was a gang. I told my team, "Come on, let's go up there and introduce ourselves." So, we went up there and I said, "Hey guys, how are things going?" We talked a little bit and I said, "How about if we all pray?" We joined hands with them and prayed.

Afterward, they seemed to be in shock they had done that. A couple days later we were doing some rehab work, and one of the gang members came up to me and said, "We know what you guys are about, and you guys are protected. We are going to

174

protect you." And except for this one bad episode with a guy from out of town, we have been protected. It has been amazing. Our relationship with the community has been phenomenal. One of the things I have been able to do is accept them just the way they are. I love these people.

Carl: But there are so many people who say you don't belong here. You and the others who make the core of this ministry are white, Anglo-Saxon, and middle class and yet ...

Bob: That is the first time I have heard that. It doesn't even cross my mind that there are different cultures here. We accept all no matter what culture they are from. If they are prostitutes, drug dealers, or doing drugs, I know who they are, but it is okay. We love on each one of them and accept them just the way they are. I know on my side of the block I try to make a point of making contact with handshakes, hugs, or even a kiss on the cheek just to let them know we love them right where they are.

Carl: Has anything you have attempted to do in this ministry not been successful?

Allen: I think we have failed a lot. I know I have. Every time we have failed, it has been because we have done what we wanted to do and not because of what God has done. When you meet someone and you try to twist that relationship to make it progress faster than it does naturally. You invite them to church and ... I think about the first dozen times someone agreed to go to church with me, and I drove up here to pick them up on Sunday morning and they didn't show. They would be in the house and they wouldn't even open the door. It was a failure because of my expectations and impatience. I expected things to happen quickly. I didn't think I had to wait on God, but what I discovered is that Jesus makes a way.

Yeah, we don't look like a lot of the people here. We live in a different cultural atmosphere. But a lot of the people here are just like us. Their circumstances are different. They have less resources a lot of the time than we do but, in terms of the difficulties of life and the things that plague them … they are addicted. I'm addicted too. I'm just addicted to different things. I am as broken as they are. Sometimes I don't do relationships well, especially with my family. I struggle with relating to my family, because I was raised in a family that didn't relate, and I didn't know how to do that. Yeah, we fail a lot. But at the same time, we have seen a lot of success.

We have seen a lot of people who have been influenced. They may not have changed the way we wanted them to change, but we can see change. Every time I think about some failure on the block, I think about the success we have seen in our team. When you put yourself in the position of giving with no expectation of anything in return, you begin to understand what the true love of God is and you begin to see God qualities and the character of Christ in the people you serve with—even the people you didn't particularly like at first.

I think people need to be in a group like this, serving like this, to fully understand the joy of working for God. Before I did this, when I heard of serving, it sounded like a chore to me. It sounded like work to me. It sounded distasteful. But I can tell you, it wasn't long after coming here and being part of Adopt-A-Block there was something that drew me. We were giving without getting anything in return.

Being a part of this ministry has changed me forever, and I am late in life. I am at that age when people don't change, yet I have been dramatically transformed. The more I am transformed, the more I am praying for stuff I never prayed for before. Now I am praying God will help me not like sports as much, and I would never have prayed that prayer even two or three years ago. The reason I don't want to be thinking about sports is because I want to be thinking about what God is doing and what is going on in this neighborhood and helping here.

176

Bob: Over the years, with all the seeds we have planted, we will probably never see the crop from that. But we see the change in people's attitude. When they see us coming, they know our names, and they know this is the church house. They know we are here for only one reason: because we love Jesus Christ. We don't evangelize by shoving it down their throats. We bring the Word and offer the love of Jesus through us. We ask them simple questions like, how can we help you today? Or, do you have any concerns we can pray for? Most of the time they do have requests, and we pray for them. Sometimes they offer the prayer and we pray with them. That was totally unheard of at the beginning. Holy Cow. We see the turnaround.

We might not see the fruit, but the fruit might come from the next generation like the boys we serve on Fridays. We have a ministry to ten to fifteen-year-old boys on Friday nights. The boys are like sponges. We only have five to eight boys, but we see them sucking it all in. They want the new life that is being offered to them.

Carl: I don't see people getting involved in a ministry like this unless they have experienced brokenness in their own life. I feel like this is so outside the Culture of Success, to borrow a phrase from my book, that I don't see becoming part of this unless God has done something to break you. Would you say that has been your experience?

Bob: I have experienced that firsthand, and I am still going through it. Almost fifty years ago I was in combat in Vietnam. There was a bad situation. Without realizing it, PTSD has caused damage to me and to my relationship with my wife, so for the past forty-seven years it has been a struggle being married. I don't know how many times I have thought I can't deal with this. I have thought about suicide twice. The only thing that saved me was God telling me "Don't do it! Don't do it!"

177

Being involved with this team ... this team is my family. I can express all my internal feelings and be prayed for and be loved on. You know you are not going to get this everywhere. I can guarantee that. It has saved my life, and it has helped my marriage. Now after fifty years of having a problem I can admit I have had a problem. I got medical help which sent me to counseling. I have been going to counseling for five years now. Fortunately, I am in the right kind of counseling.

With this ministry, I am being extremely selfish. It has saved my life and brought a light to my heart only God can give. There are days I don't want to come. I have been doing this so long. As soon as I walk in these doors, however, and I am here with my family, the family of Jesus Christ, what a difference. I am more comfortable here than with my own family. My daughter and my granddaughters are not believers in Jesus Christ in the fashion I wish they were. It breaks my heart, but I come here and I receive so much. I am being so selfish to say that, but it is the truth.

Allen: It is the most unusual dynamic.

Carl: How would you say God has used brokenness in your own life, Allen, to prepare you for this?

Allen: My brokenness wasn't evident. I was very good at hiding it. I was very frustrated because I knew, while I understood the Word of God very clearly, it wasn't working the way it needed to in my life. I came to the point where I said, "I don't want to do what I am doing any more." I didn't feel like it was real. I didn't feel like it was genuine. I mean, I loved God and I loved the people I was serving, but my motivations were all screwed up. I was trying to hang on to a place and maintain who I was and the image I wanted people to have of me. At the same time, I was not a good dad or a good husband. It seemed like it on the surface, and it seemed like it to me. When I was really honest, however, I would have to admit it wasn't good. I believed totally in the spiritual life, but it wasn't working that well for me. It looked like it was, but it wasn't.

Coming to Adopt-A-Block and beginning to love the people and serving without expecting anything ... you let the walls down. You let the barriers down. You become completely non-defensive. You just give up. You say, "The only chance I have in the world is for God to change me." I can't change myself. It takes the Spirit of God.

In the last four years I look the same. I sound the same. But I am not the same. I have been transformed by service. For years I couldn't understand why people wanted to go to Bible conferences. I didn't need to learn more about God, because I wasn't using what I already knew. I wasn't living up to what I knew. Coming on the block and serving with people this closely in this kind of an environment, you begin to learn who they really are and, when you bring your barriers down, they learn who you really are. I could never understand why Jesus would value me, and now I understand. It is totally unmerited. I thought I understood it before, but I really didn't. I have known what to do in order to do Christianity for a long time. What I realize I really need now is to know God Himself.

Without Jesus Christ, I don't have the motivation to do what I do, and I feel like an Old Testament guy who doesn't have the Spirit drawing me. Now, even on days when I don't feel like coming up here, I sense the Spirit of God drawing me to come. He is shaping me and molding me, and I cannot even explain how that makes me feel. My peace and joy have nothing to do with my external surroundings. I can see God changing me and because I can see God is changing me, I can go and knock on that door. I know if God can change me, He can change anyone.

Carl: Well, gentlemen, thank you very much for your time. I knew there was something special with Adopt-A-Block one of my first weeks here when a policeman told me your ministry has changed this neighborhood. I thought that was an amazing statement for a policeman to say.

Allen: I can see the change. Not so much with the adults, but since we have been pouring into these kids. I can see the change in these kids. We have kids who come to the ministry house to help others and give their time in service. We have kids who come here just to hang out with us. What makes ten to fourteen-year-old boys want to hang out with seventy-year-old men?

Carl: Don't discount the impact you have had on adults either. Last week when I was here, we were walking down the road when a woman came out and began talking to Bob. She opened up her heart as she talked about the abuse she was suffering and the pain she was going through. Bob, you heard more in that short conversation about that woman's life situation than most pastors know about their congregation of fifteen years. Your impact is built on your relationship with the people here and the men God is making you. Thank you, gentlemen, for your time, your honesty, and your ministry.

Author's Note: AAB in York is a ministry of the York Regional Dream Center, a collaborative subsidiary of Grace Fellowship Church of Shrewsbury, Pennsylvania. They host a variety of weekly ministries and make regular block visits. The York Regional Dream Center is inspired by the Los Angeles Dream Center.

Meditation Moment

- Many people choose to go to church because they like the preaching, music, and friendly people. In the early church, gathering together with believers was the most dangerous thing a person could do. For hundreds of years, every time Christians gathered together they risked discovery, arrest, beatings, and death. Even today, believers around the world, such as the Egyptian churches attacked on a recent Palm Sunday, are willing to die to worship with other believers. Why do people place such a high value on gathering together? What is so important that it drives people to take such risks?

- Every church has its own personality. Every church has its own priorities and passions. Every church has its own problem areas where people might feel left out or even be hurt. Have you ever been hurt or disappointed by a church? If so, how did you react and what did you learn from the experience?

- Before Jesus ascended to heaven after his resurrection, He left the church with a mission.

All authority has been given to Me in heaven and on earth. Go therefore and make disciples of all the nations, baptizing them in the name of the Father and the Son and the Holy Spirit, teaching them to observe all that I commanded you; and lo, I am with you always, even to the end of the age (Matthew 28:18-20).

The Ministry of Failure is a road map to life with a clear purpose and an abiding sense of God's presence. It is a journey God wants us to travel with other imperfect people. Disciples are people who are learning—people who are working with each other and with God to figure out how to live life successfully. Are you willing to join Jesus in this mission?

Chapter Ten

The End of the Matter

Everyone wants their story to end well.

"The end of a matter is better than its beginning; patience of spirit is better than haughtiness of spirit" (Ecclesiastes 7:8).

Miami Southridge High School won the state football championship in 2016. If I hadn't moved to Virginia in the middle of my senior year, I would have been part of the first graduating class Miami Southridge ever had (class of 1978). In 1977, our football season also started off with dreams of a championship season, but then our coach was arrested. We got a new head coach in the middle of the season. The transition did not go well. While several heartbreaking losses meant we had no hope of playing for the championship, the last game of the year meant a great deal to me personally since it was against a powerhouse school, Miami Palmetto, which I attended my freshman year. As we prepared to start the game, I learned several of our linemen were drunk, and I knew our season would not end well.

Everyone wants their story to end well. Whether it does or not often depends on where we stop the story. My football story ended in our defeat against Miami Palmetto. Several of my teammates went on to play in college, and one eventually played in the NFL. God never intends the Ministry of Failure to end with our story in defeat. If we follow biblical principles, there can always be the victory of a lesson learned, a bad habit lost, a relationship healed, a new perspective gained, a sin confessed, grace received, a testimony given, or a life saved. We miss blessings when we end the story prematurely so we can go back to the Culture of Success.

Even though my last pastorate, Hope Fellowship, worked through its time of conflict, a year of introspection had taken a numerical toll. The church slowly atrophied to the size it was when I first arrived. Even though the church was also healthier than it had been in a long time, the decision was eventually made to join with another church which had begun leasing Hope's old church building. We folded and joined our resources to this sister church.

My final point in my final sermon to Hope Fellowship was based on the end of time. Matthew 25 tells us that one day Jesus will come to separate everyone who has ever lived into two groups. These two groups will face radically different fates.

The first group is blessed for their service without reference to sin (Matthew 25:34-40).

The second group is judged for their sin without reference to blessing (Matthew 25:41-45).

As I was contemplating on this passage with Hope Fellowship in their last service, I pointed out that people would look at us and say, "Well, Hope Fellowship is a failure. It is history." And from the Culture of Success' perspective, these critics would be right. The problem with this perspective is the fact that at the Final Judgment, everything is history. Every church, every nation and civilization, every job, every family, every relationship, every struggle, every failure, and every success will be history as we stand before God. History, in fact, is all that will exist as the basis for our reward or punishment. Hope Fellowship's history of ministry is not eliminated. It is just completed. The history of the former members continues while serving in other churches.

Peter is a wonderful example of the fact that as long as we are on this earth, our history is still being written. After the crucifixion of Jesus, Peter returned to the family business of fishing. One day while fishing, he had an encounter with his resurrected Friend. Much has been made of the fact that Peter denied Jesus three times and, here on a beach, Jesus gave Peter three opportunities to profess his love. While there was undoubtedly symbolism in this restoration for Peter, there was a more important meaning in this dialogue (see John 21:15-17).

Jesus' questioning of Peter placed Peter in an awkward position which must have been very humbling. It hadn't been that long since Peter declared his willingness to follow Jesus to the death. "Jesus, I know I declared my absolute dedication to You right before I disappointed You, lied to You, abandoned You, and denied You, but I really love you today," would have been a very difficult conversation. Fortunately, Jesus accepted Peter's love without any reference to their recent past. Peter repented in tears and, after the resurrection, there is no record of Jesus discussing it.

Instead, Jesus affirmed Peter and helped him move on. After each love declaration, "Feed my sheep" gave Peter tacit permission to be a human being who has failed and yet has been called for ministry. Rather than disqualifying him for ministry, the Ministry of Failure gave Peter the honest perspective and humility he needed to be used by God in a mighty way.

But Peter's journey would not be easy. After the third profession, Jesus told Peter that as an old man Peter would be bound up and taken "where you don't want to go." Jesus then told Peter, "Follow Me" (vs. 18-19).

Peter, having just returned to the comfortable world of fishing, was clearly overwhelmed by this new calling to follow Jesus no matter the cost. Turning to John, Peter tried to deflect Jesus' focus by asking, "Lord, and what about this man?" Jesus

184

responded by saying, "If I want him to remain until I come, what is that to you? You follow Me!" (vs. 21-22).

In other words, if you want your story to end well, don't worry about what other people are doing, "You follow Me!" Fortunately for us, Peter did so. He became a powerful leader in the early church and preached the first Church's sermon at Pentecost where three thousand people came to faith in Jesus. He healed the sick and raised the dead. He traveled extensively sharing the gospel and wrote two books of the New Testament.

Tradition says Peter was eventually taken "where you do not want to go" and was crucified upside down for his faith in Jesus. While you and I may not want to die in such a painful way, one thing is for certain, Peter's life story ended well.

While Peter's story is powerful, there is another person in the Bible who could serve as the poster child for failure. By the time he appears in Scripture, this person had long before given up trying to live up to the Culture of Success' expectations. In all likelihood, his family had disowned him, and all his friends were dismal failures as well. The Bible describes him simply as a thief, but even in this chosen career he was a failure.

Arrested by the Romans, he and a fellow criminal were sentenced to die by crucifixion. Initially, as he suffered on his cross, this thief turned his anger and pain onto Jesus, who was being crucified at the same time. Seeing everyone mock Jesus as a king, he couldn't resist joining in and dishing out some of the pain and humiliation he was feeling. As time went on, though, he saw something different in this man, and he became silent as the verbal abuse around him continued.

Finally, hearing his partner in crime hurling abuse at Jesus, the failed thief could stand it no more. He shouted "Do you not even fear God, since you are under the same sentence of condemnation? And we indeed are suffering justly, for we are receiving what we deserve for our deeds; but this man has done nothing wrong" (Luke 23:40-41).

As if his change of heart wasn't shocking enough, what he did next was truly stunning. He turned to Jesus and said, "Jesus, remember me when You come in Your kingdom!" (vs. 42). Somehow through the fog of his own agonizing death, he saw Jesus for who He was. As if Jesus was waiting for this moment, Jesus didn't even hesitate to answer his plea. "Truly I say to you, today you shall be with Me in Paradise" (vs. 43).

As I was writing this chapter, I was meditating on this passage about the thief on the cross for a couple hours as I prepared for and went to church. Our church has two wonderful teaching pastors, Pastor Ben and Pastor Jason. Imagine my surprise when Pastor Ben stood up and preached on this passage which had been on my heart all morning. At the conclusion of his sermon, Ben said:

Let me ask this question. If, in one hundred thousand years from today, we asked this convert on the cross, "What was the best day of your life?" what do you think he would say?

"Mr. Criminal, I read about your story. I read about your change of heart. Is it fair to say that it was an expensive and painful lesson?"

"Yes," he would say, "Yes, it was expensive and painful."

"And, Mr. Criminal, would you change it? Would you have it another way?"

"Never," he would say. "Never would I want it another way."

The thief on the cross reminds me of one of my brothers-in-law. From the time I met him, my future brother-in-law had no interest in God. As far as I could tell, he only had two passions, my sister and drinking. After I became a Christian, he made a point of asking me to do things I obviously would not or should never do. He seemed to believe Christianity was something to be mocked more than something to ascribe to. As he got older, drinking became less important to him and his family and friends more. While the mocking stopped, and he professed to believe in God, he shunned anything dealing with church.

In 2016, my brother-in-law began losing weight. In three months, he mysteriously lost over fifty pounds. It wasn't long before he was diagnosed with stage four aggressive cancer. When he called and asked me to come meet with him about becoming a Christian, I went as soon as I could. As we talked, I told him about the convert on the cross and asked if he was ready to make the same appeal to God. He didn't hesitate to say he was. Bowing his head, he said a simple prayer asking God for forgiveness and committing his life to Jesus.

I explained to him that being baptized meant joining a church, and he said he was happy to do so. At his baptism a couple weeks later, he was so weak it took three grown men to get him into the baptismal. When I asked him if there was anything he wanted to share with his friends and family, he declared how much each of us needs God. It was a profession he stayed true to for the remaining weeks of his life. Like the thief on the cross, any life that ends following Jesus ends well.

Fortunately, we do not have to wait until the end of life to benefit from the Ministry of Failure. Every time our shortcomings and failures lead us to experience the grace and mercy of God, we are blessed.

A few years ago, there was an explosion of noise from the lunchroom. Tables and chairs were being thrown. Kids were screaming. Another teacher and I sprinted down the stairs to support whoever was doing lunch duty. By the time we arrived, the fight was over, the responsible student was restrained, and other teachers had the remaining kids under control. That was over two years and two surgeries ago. I severely injured my right foot and ankle in my rush to get to the cafeteria.

While you might assume my injury was a result of my noble quest to stop a fight, the truth is I was leaping down the stairs to beat a female teacher who was also rushing down to respond. My doctor tells me my foot—injured as a direct result of my chauvinistic pride—will never be pain-free. Unless God performs a miracle, this disability is a consequence I have to live with. It has also brought me to a deeper understanding of my dependence on God than I have ever had before.

In the book of Job, one of Job's friends told him while he was in the depths of his pain, "Yield now and be at peace with Him; thereby good will come to you" (Job 22:21). Sounds good, but for people who are suffering loss or failure it is not always comforting.

I know a sailor who suffered a major back injury at work. After having his spine fused, he continued to have extreme pain. His doctor suspected him of drug addiction and told him his pain was psychological and no further treatment would be provided. His neighbor across the street came to visit and told him if he would just get right with God, God would remove the pain. Later, it was determined that the fusion had failed, and the man was walking around with a broken back. The man did not need condemnation or platitudes. He needed the pieces of his spine put back together.

There are times in life when we need to know the pieces of our failure can be put together for some ultimate good. People sometimes condemn and sometimes reject us in our failure. Sometimes they misapply Scripture to our detriment. Sometimes people take the high road and lovingly provide guidance, accountability, and encouragement which helps us move past our failure. God's response goes beyond any human intervention.

Only God can put the pieces of our failure together and change our world in ways we can't imagine.

The uniqueness of God's reaction to failure is reflective of the eternal cry of beings around the throne of God calling out, "Holy, Holy, Holy, is the Lord of hosts" (Isaiah 6:3). The word holy means other, and the triple repetition means God is more unlike anyone else than any other. It is an amazing declaration from beings with six wings each and, according to the book of Revelation, full of eyes around and within. Beings more unusual than we can possibly imagine are declaring God is the most unusual being in the universe. God is holy, and it should not surprise us that He can demonstrate His love, understanding, and power in unique ways we cannot fathom, turning something disappointing and painful into something special.

I once went to a church with a quilting ministry. On one rack was the ugliest mess of a quilt I had ever seen, until someone turned it over and I saw the other side. It was beautiful. In this life, you and I are creating threads woven into a tapestry. Each thread is a long string of failures held together and given a unique color by the grace of God. Any part of our life which is not failure is the grace of God. Sometimes, though, it seems like these strings are just making a mess. In truth, one day we will see the other side of the tapestry where I imagine a vast plane of yellow with the words, "Hallelujah! To God be the glory!" embroidered by the grace of God in a near infinitely diverse panorama of colors.

People have shared pieces of their life threads as they exist to date in this book. It is to date because each of us is called to continue following God as long as we live. Your thread is unique to who you are, has brought you to where you are, and is leading you to future appointments with God. All we need to do to discover these powerful life-changing experiences is to obey the words of Jesus, "Follow Me!"

189

While this may sound simple, this obedience is seldom an easy journey, and it will inevitably take us out of our comfort zone, requiring us to change our patterns of behavior and learn new ways to seek success and avoid failure. It will challenge our very understanding of what success looks like and affect our ambitions, desires, and dreams. It is also the reason for which we were created.

A common theme of many self-help books is to avoid identifying yourself as a failure. We don't mind admitting we fail occasionally, but we emotionally balk at identifying ourselves as less than ultimately successful. If you doubt this, ask yourself why the word wretch in the hymn "Amazing Grace" has been changed in some modern hymn books.

Wretches don't fit in the Culture of Success.

While no one wakes up in the morning aspiring to be a wretch, the idea of being a wretch in the eyes of the world is somehow less problematic when you realize you really don't belong in this world. As Paul said, "our citizenship is in heaven" (Philippians 3:20).

It currently costs $725 to become a citizen of the United States. There is a $640 application fee and an $85 background check cost. It has also cost the blood, sweat, and tears of countless Americans and patriots who have sacrificed for our right to be an American. Our eternal citizenship may not come with an application fee, but it does come with a background check and a high price—a background check and a higher price than any poor wretch could ever pass or pay. Fortunately, the bloody price for our heavenly citizenship was paid by Jesus on the cross, and His followers are the recipients of His priceless grace. As such, our eternal background check now comes back simply as: child of God.

In chapter six of this book, I mentioned I spent a summer vacation in Liberia. I actually went to Liberia two summers in a row. The first summer my brother, Alan, was also able to visit. My brother was six-feet-four and very strong. Nothing scared him. A few days after we arrived in Liberia, Alan went for a walk without telling anyone where he was going. After he came home from his walk, men from the American embassy came to our apartment and escorted Alan to see the American ambassador. It seems someone had seen him walking through the worst slum in Monrovia.

In no uncertain terms, the ambassador informed my brother that he was not a native of Liberia, and he was never to walk through the slums of Monrovia on his own again. By doing so, he risked not only his health and freedom (kidnapping was common), he risked our family's happiness and my father's security as an employee of the CIA.

As a child of God, you no more belong in the Culture of Success than Alan belonged in the slums of Monrovia. When we try to make ourselves at home in the world's expectations, we endanger not only our spiritual health but the joy of everyone around us and the well-being of our Father's mission here on this earth.

It is our heavenly citizenship which allows us to look beyond the Culture of Success and joyfully accept the limitations of this life. You are a wretch, but you are a wretch who is blessed by a loving God with infinite worth and eternal value as His adopted child. This humble perspective opens the door for a grateful heart and a bond of grace with all men.

When properly understood, the Ministry of Failure provides us with the ability to look beyond people's failures (including our own) and see the image of God, giving us a new love for God and for others. This love then becomes our motivation to live lives foreign to the Culture of Success and through which God can impact others. "By this all men will know that you are My disciples, if you have love for one another" (John 13:35).

While our testimony is an important tool God wants to use to His glory, love speaks even louder than words. I Corinthians 13:4-8 describes love in powerful terms.

Love is patient, love is kind and is not jealous; love does not brag and is not arrogant, does not act unbecomingly; it does not seek its own, is not provoked, does not take into account a wrong suffered, does not rejoice in unrighteousness, but rejoices with the truth; bears all things, believes all things, hopes all things, endures all things.

Love never fails ...

Love is the ultimate success story. It is the source and the end of the Ministry of Failure.

Your Story

_____
_____
_____
_____
_____
_____
_____
_____
_____
_____
_____
_____
_____
_____
_____
_____
_____
_____
_____
_____
_____
_____
_____
_____

Meditation Moment

- What does "ending your life well" mean to you? Imagine your final judgment. What history do you want to be forgotten? What history do you want to take with you? (This is the grace given the sheep at the final judgment. Only the good remains.)

- As a result of the Ministry of Failure in your own life, what life changes is God calling you to make? How will these changes affect the people around you? Are you willing to do whatever it takes to obey God's call?

- To say we love someone or something doesn't mean anything without a context, because the word love means many things. I love my wife and I love my cat. Jesus and Peter both used specific words to describe Peter's love for Jesus. Would you say you love Jesus? If so, what kind of love do you love Him with today?

- Success and failure are a matter of comparison to a standard. What is your standard of success? Are you willing to let the description of love in I Corinthians 13:4-8 discussed at the end of this last chapter be your new standard of success?

- What have you learned from the Ministry of Failure? The last testimony in this book is yours to write. If you would be willing to share your story on my Facebook page or if you have any insights or questions, please email me at Godovercomes@gmail.com.

Endnotes

Chapter Three

[1]acton.org/press/release/2006/charles-w-colson-receive-acton-institutes-faith-fr

[2]www.christianitytoday.com/ct/2012/aprilweb-only/chuck-colson-dead.html

[3]Summary by the Clark County, Indiana Prosecutor's Office based on Texas Court of Criminal Appeals case, Tucker v. State, 771 S.W.2d 523 (Tex.Cr.App. 1988).

[4]For the full interview, see edition.cnn.com/2007/US/03/21/larry.king.tucker/index.html?iref=mpstoryview

[5]www.beliefnet.com/faiths/christianity/2004/10/charles-stanley-satan-always-attacks-the-mind.aspx#FQqex82XvAzVY4AC.99

Chapter Four

[6]Matthew Henry's Commentary on the Whole Bible, vol. 6. Public Domain.

[7]C.S. Lewis, Mere Christianity, MacMillan Publishing Co., New York, 1952, p. 111.

Chapter Five

8http://www.thepublicdiscourse.com/2015/12/15983

[9]Richard Cory by Edwin Arlington Robinson, pub. 1897.

Chapter Six

[10]Adapted from a sermon by Dr. James Allan Francis in "The Real Jesus and Other Sermons" © 1926 by the Judson Press of Philadelphia.

[11]Pastor Rick's Daily Hope, May 21, 2014: Our Inheritance: Grace, Patience, Wisdom, And Power

Chapter Eight

[12]Improving Fluid Intelligence with Training on Working Memory, Jaeggi, Buschkuehl, Jonides, and Perrig, © 2008 by The National Academy of Sciences of the USA, published online May 13, 2008.